ACQUIRING BALL SKILL

ACQUIRING BALL SKILL

A Psychological Interpretation

*

H. T. A. WHITING
M.A., Ph.D., D.L.C.

Department of Physical Education,
University of Leeds

LEA & FEBIGER
Philadelphia

Contents

		page
Preface		vii

1. INTRODUCTION — 1
   Systems-Analysis of Perceptual Motor Skill Performance — 2
   Display — 4
   Perception — 4
   Selective Attention — 6
   Feedback — 6
   Categories of Ball Skills — 8
   'Open' and 'Closed' Skills — 9

2. INPUT CHARACTERISTICS — 12
   Information Processing — 14
   Predicting Ball Flight — 17
   Experimental Findings — 19
   Perceptual Units — 28
   Conclusions — 34

3. DECISION MAKING — 36
   Simple Reaction Time — 36
   Transit Reaction Time — 41
   Choice Reaction Time — 44
   Psychological Refractoriness — 48

4. OUTPUT CHARACTERISTICS — 55
   Replicability — 58
   Efferent Information — 60

5. VISUAL FACTORS — 62
   Depth Perception — 65
   Eye Dominance — 67
   Peripheral Vision — 69

6. ACQUIRING SKILL IN BALL GAMES   72
   'Imitation' in acquiring Ball Skill   74
   Discrimination   79
   'Guidance' in Skill Learning   80
   Speed or Accuracy   81
   Mental Practice   82

7. INDIVIDUAL DIFFERENCES   84
   Personality Assessment   85
   Experimental Findings   89
   Personality and Perception   96
   Abilities and Performance   99

8 SUMMARY   102

   Acknowledgements   106
   References   108
   Subject Index   116

Plates

Between pages 38 and 39

   1. The display to a car-driver
   2. The display to a badminton player
 3-6. The golfer's swing
   7. Keep your eye on the ball? Adult
   8. Keep your eye on the ball? Child
9-12. The difficulty experienced by a young child in catching
       a ball
13-14. Differences in inter-pupillary distances

Preface

Ball games are big business! They occupy the playing time of millions of people throughout the world and the watching time of countless more. Top professional players earn large sums of money, spectators contribute massive financial support to their teams and international tournaments are arranged in which monetary expenditure is often of little object. Even international prestige centres around the results of European, Asian, American and World competition! In spite of the continued outflow of time, money and energy, the coaching of ball games remains an art. A sophisticated art it is true, but an art nevertheless. The amount of time and money spent on research investigations into ball skill acquisition or the psychological, sociological and physiological effects of games playing is trivial.

This book sets out to review the experimental literature which does exist with a view to its application in the acquisition of ball skill. In the main, such literature is not from the field of sport since what is written in such books is generally subjective or related to the attainment of success by particular players or teams. This is not to deny that sports writers have not been aware of many of the issues raised but, so far, there does not seem to have been a book published which is devoted to an objective view of the important factors in the acquisition of ball skill in general.

Perhaps the most numerous body of people concerned with the teaching of ball games are those in the physical education profession (although it is worth noting, and may be of significance, that those concerned with introducing children to the initial stages of ball game skill will not be specialist trained teachers of games). Although such people are concerned with the *training* of players for ball games, they are also educationalists. This necessarily means, that they have wider considerations than the development of ball-game playing ability in their children to the exclusion of all else. Such teachers will be concerned with and may put primary emphasis on the social, emotional and recreative aspects of games participation in addition to any skill development which may take place. They may be using games as a means of education in which the attainment of a high level of proficiency is incidental. In spite of such considerations, the cult of the school team and the prestige that success carries, will often mean that with some children at least, training in top level ball skill is a fundamental consideration.

It is this two-fold approach—*training* in ball games and *education* through the medium of ball games—that bedevils the methodology of instruction. In saying this, it is not intended to put a value judgement on either of these procedures but it does mean that considerations for one of these approaches may not be suitable for the other. Without therefore being in any way critical about the process of education through games (an approach to which I would subscribe), such considerations will be of secondary importance throughout this book. The primary consideration will be with some of the principles involved in the *training* of ball-game players. Nevertheless, the principles involved are considered to be basic to physical educationalists, coaches, teachers, players and to the more sophisticated spectator.

If there is one principle which has become reasonably well established in the experimental analysis of human performance, it is the *specificity* of skilled behaviour. By this statement is meant that if success is to be attained in a particular skill area, extended practice in *that* area is a prerequisite. If this principle is accepted, then the training of ball players outside the game situation must be viewed with caution and all concerned with such procedures must be clear on what they are trying to achieve by such methods. An appreciation of this problem is perhaps illustrated by current training procedures which attempt to make ball skill practices taken out of the context of the game as near as possible to the game situation. In so doing, the coach is making the assumption that transfer of training from the 'mini' situation to the full game will be brought about by such a procedure. He may well be right. Although the literature on transfer of training is considerable,

the exact nature of transfer in any situation is far from well
defined. This has led Meredith (1966) to comment that:

> . . . the statistical facts of transfer are so dependent on the
> educational context that they are too diffuse to be capable of
> precise investigation except in carefully specified circum-
> stances.

If, however, the evidence amassed by experimental psychologists such as Osgood (1953) is considered, it will be found that
while maximum facilitation as would be expected, occurs when
both stimulus and response situations are functionally identical,
transfer effects fall off as the degree of similarity between stimuli
and responses in the two tasks differ. In this context, the
relationship between practice and game conditions must be
very carefully considered. A similar principle is involved in
Holding's (1962) concept of 'inclusion' in relation to transfer
effects from difficult-easy and easy-difficult situations. This
suggests, that where a subskill has been practised out of the
context of a skill complex, positive transfer from the easy to the
difficult task might be expected. It must, however, again be
asked how close in terms of both perceptual and motor characteristics is the subskill when practised outside the game situation
to what is supposed to be the subskill within the game itself?

If such considerations raise difficult problems for skill
sequences supposedly extracted from the game and practised in
near game situations, how much more difficult it is to justify the
practice of isolated skills if eventually it is the game itself in
which primary interest lies. What purpose is served for
example by chest-passing in pairs across the gymnasium for
potential basketball players or stationary passes in hockey for
budding hockey players? What is happening when children
are allowed to deliberately go for rallies when learning racquet
games? True, it maintains their interest (which may be of
fundamental importance), but in as far as in games competition
the purpose is not to have rallies, it is necessary to justify the
former procedure for achieving the latter. Perhaps education
and training are again being confused in this context?

Unfortunately, evidence is sparse for any of the procedures
suggested and as in education in general, method follows current
fashion and myths can easily be perpetuated. Circular reason-
ing does not help in this situation. Because a certain amount

of success is achieved by a given method, it does not mean that
it is the best or only method although it may be sufficient
justification for the teacher or coach in control. So many
things lead to success. The really enthusiastic teacher with
little technical knowledge can achieve quite outstanding team
results *just* by the interest he takes in the team he is with.

What all this amounts to, is that little is really known about
'how' to teach ball games in the most successful and efficient
way, or whether methods should differ at different ages and
with differing abilities. Teachers and coaches learn from their
teachers and coaches—methods of approach are perpetuated.
Results of some kind or other are achieved and accepted.
There is a need to question fundamental approaches, to initiate
investigations to clarify some of the issues and above all for
teachers and coaches to be aware of possibilities. As stated at
the beginning of this preface, many of the problems are
imposed by philosophical considerations which need to be
resolved before methods of teaching/coaching can be justified.
It is not intended to develop this theme any further, suffice it for
the reader to understand that it is the *training* of ball skills that
is being considered here.

The book is designed to establish a basic model for skill in the
first chapter. Subsequent chapters develop particular systems
of the model in relation to the acquisition of ball-game skill.
Throughout the book, references are given which enable the
interested reader to follow up particular topics which have
received only a limited treatment. In this way, the book will
be of particular interest to students in training and should serve
as a source of reference from College of Education level to
higher degree work.

Leeds 1968   H. T. A. Whiting

CHAPTER 1

Introduction

The decision to restrict the scope of this book to ball* skills can be misleading since the reader may form an impression that such skills are entirely in a class of their own. While the presence of a ball—particularly of a ball in flight—adds important considerations to the acquisition of such skills, it is worth stressing that similar models have been suggested for skills in many different categories. Welford (1958) for example talks about the acquisition of *motor* skills and Argyle & Kendon (1967) about the acquisition of *social* skills from similar viewpoints. Thus, two seemingly diverse categories of skills have been analysed in similar ways. But even here, a decision to classify skills as *motor* or *social*, while being useful from the point of view of emphasising the observed behaviour with which different workers are primarily concerned, can be misleading in as far as it focusses attention on a limited area of the whole skill sequence. The current trend is rather to consider all skills as perceptual-motor thereby stressing the important relationship which exists between input and output data in their performance. To Welford and Argyle & Kendon, such a proposition is axiomatic. Throughout this book, the prefix 'perceptual-motor' will likewise be assumed to apply to the skills discussed even when not specifically stated. In this respect, a *skill* has been defined by Argyle & Kendon (1967) as:

> . . . an organised, coordinated activity in relation to an object or a situation which involves a whole chain of sensory, central and motor mechanisms.

Knapp (1964) has also drawn the distinction between 'skill' and 'a skill'. The former she defines as:

> . . . the learned ability to bring about predetermined results with maximum certainty often with the minimum outlay of time or energy or both.

* Hereafter, the word 'ball' will be taken to stand for ball, shuttlecock, puck, etc.

It might therefore be useful to think in terms of more or less skilful players in one or more ball skills. Since any of the major games (football, hockey, golf, lacrosse, etc.) involve a variety of ball *skills*, it is to be expected that individual players may be *skilful* in some or all of these skills and since more than one player is usually involved, social skills may also be important.

Systems-Analysis of Perceptual-Motor Skill Performance

The use of models of human performance serves as an aid to the understanding of the function of such a complex system as the human body. The 'systems approach' to model building abstracts the common procedures from amongst the multitudinous acts of behaviour and categorises them as components in which their function may be more easily understood. By such techniques, an attempt is made to determine the relative functioning of subsystems of such components with respect to the entire system. An approach of this nature will be used in relation to perceptual-motor skill and built up in four stages. While not being the only model put forward as an aid to the study of skill acquisition, it has the merit of simplicity, particularly in elaborating important concepts.   In a later chapter it will be necessary to introduce an 'information theory' model. Other useful models have been reviewed by Fitts (1964).

In terms of the *physical* components of human perceptual-motor performance, it is useful to consider first of all a simple model—Figure 1—representing the link between sense organs,

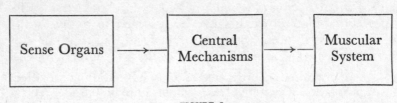

FIGURE I
Physical components

central mechanisms of the brain and the muscular system (Singleton, 1967). At a functional level such physical components give rise to the reception of *input* data via the sense organs, *decision making* in the central mechanisms and *output* data via the muscular system—Figure 2. The central mech-

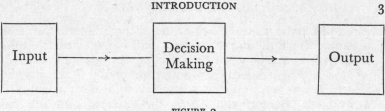

FIGURE 2
Functional components

anisms may be further elaborated in terms of the functions they are known to perform (Welford, 1960)—Figure 3. Three primary systems are recognised—*perceptual, translatory* and *effector*.

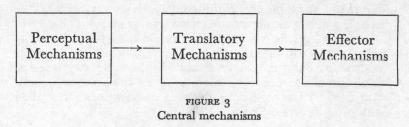

FIGURE 3
Central mechanisms

Finally, these three simple models can be incorporated to give a more complicated but at the same time more informative systems-analysis of perceptual-motor performance—Figure 4.

One of the difficulties in presenting two-dimensional models of this kind on paper is that they give the reader the idea of a static system. The nervous system of the human body is constantly active (in terms of the firing of nerve cells), the environment (both internal and external) is continually changing, attention fluctuates and man is never still. The components of the model while maintaining their overall basic structure and function are in a continuous state of change, of elaboration and sophistication. The model must be conceived as a dynamic model.

Basically, the systems' components in this composite model together with their interactions can be elaborated as follows:

Information about the *display* (immediate external environment in which the skill is to be carried out—Plates 1 and 2) or about the internal environment (proprioceptive* information)

* The kinaesthetic (receptors in the muscles, tendons and joints) and vestibular senses are sometimes collectively referred to as the proprioceptive senses (Morgan & King, 1966).

is relayed to the central mechanisms of the brain via the sense organs. Since the performer of a skill cannot utilise *all* the information available in the display at any one instant, *selective attention* determines both the area of the display which is scanned and the particular information which is abstracted. Sensory data from the external and internal environment is interpreted (the process of *perception*) in the central perceptual mechanisms. On the basis of such perceptions, decisions are made with regard to new responses or adjustments to ongoing responses. If a response is to be made, the translatory mechanism selects the appropriate response pattern and the effector system gives the executive command to appropriate muscular response systems. The carrying out of an effector response brings about a change in the display giving rise to 'feedback' information about the effectiveness of the response. Such information together with other information from the display and the internal environment can then be monitored by the sensory systems and used in the control of ongoing responses or utilised in initiating future responses.

This brief outline has introduced a number of concepts which may be new to the reader. Those which are considered to be of particular importance are elaborated briefly below. Additional information and background reading can be obtained by following up the references quoted.

Display (Plates 1 and 2)

The display is that part of the external environment which contains information which is likely to be of use—or in some cases necessary—in performance of the skill. It will be that part of the external environment towards which attention needs to be directed for the purpose of taking in information the processing of which gives rise to decision making which will affect the performance of the skill (Shackel & Whitfield, 1963).

Perception

In attempting to understand perception in relation to ball skills, it is necessary to realise that the distance receptors (eyes and ears) which play such an important part in monitoring information from the display are sensitive to incoming light or sound energy. At the receptors, such energy is converted into

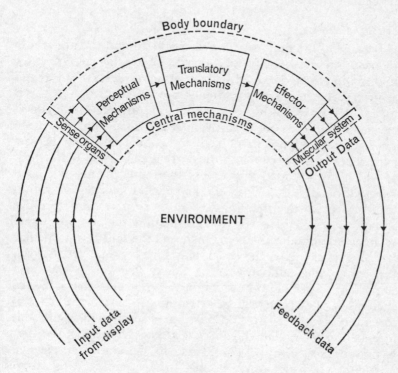

FIGURE 4

Systems analysis of perceptual-motor performance

chains of electrical impulses (neural coding) and relayed to the central mechanisms via the appropriate nerves (Gregory, 1966). It is these impulses which give rise to the patterns of brain activity the processing and interpretation of which constitute the act of perception. It is the brain which is responsible for perceiving and not the sense organs!

Selective Attention

Because of the limitations of the sense organs, the amount of information present in any display and the necessity for information to be obtained with an optimum level of speed and accuracy, it is necessary for attention to be selective. By this is meant that consciously or unconsciously, attention is focussed on particular areas of a display. Such focussing may be a random process but is more likely to be determined by the past experience of the person and the current skill being performed. It will be appreciated that one of the requirements of a good ball-skill coach is that he should know what information within a display is worth attending to, i.e. those particular stimulus situations which give rise to information the monitoring of which is essential for the performance of the skill at a particular level. For example, the coach may instruct a player to 'keep his eye on the ball' because he thinks that this is the most important source of information in the control of the skill. In such cases, the coach will be attempting to make the players' attention selective. It appears that stimuli which are not attended to are excluded from perception (Horn, 1966) so that a person may also be considered to demonstrate selective *perception*. It is also worth noting that in concentrating attention on relevant stimuli, it is necessary to ignore stimuli which are irrelevant. As Rabbitt (1967) has recently pointed out, this may equally well be a learned ability.

Feedback

Although 'feedback' is a common enough term in relation to the control of machine systems, its adoption in the description of human control systems is comparatively recent and would appear to have developed from Wiener's (1948) elaboration of Cybernetics (the science of control and communication). Although the analogy between the control of machine systems and the control of the human system is a useful one, there are important differences in the characteristics of the two systems (Milhorn, 1966). In terms of the human control system, feedback is often designated 'knowledge of results'. Holding (1966) with others distinguishes between internal and external feedback. Internal feedback—in terms of proprioceptive information—is intrinsic to all human performance. External feedback—represented by changes in the display—may be intrinsic to a particular performance in as far as it is the direct result of the action. However, it may also be provided by an external agency (such as a coach) giving rise to what has been termed *augmented knowledge of results*.

Feedback may be utilised in the control of ongoing responses (action feedback) or it may be retained in memory store and used in the control of subsequent responses (learning feedback). Thus, information about the result of hitting a ball will be monitored by a player and such information used to help in the control of either ongoing movements—as in dribbling a hockey ball—or future movements of a similar kind.

If the 'black-box'* model given in Figure 4 is considered useful in analysing the components of a skilled action, it may also be found useful to look for breakdown in skilled performance in one or more of these mechanisms and their related feedback. While a breakdown in skilled performance will always manifest itself in inadequate or inappropriate motor behaviour, it does not follow that there is necessarily any deficiency in the *effector* system. A number of subsystems contribute to total effective performance. For example, in performing a ball skill, a player may fail to select the important information from the display. On the other hand, he may focus his attention on the right area of the display but put a wrong interpretation on the data conveyed via the sense organs to the central perceptual mechanisms. Correspondingly, the right perceptual interpretation might be put on appropriate sensory input but an inappropriate response might be selected. Finally, there may be a failure on the effector side in terms of such variables as timing, effort, or feedback control of ongoing movements.

An analysis of a situation in these terms may lead a player or

* The 'black-box' approach to modelling is in terms of a system which will account for all the known responses. It is used because in general, interactions of variables inside the black box are not known (Milhorn, 1966).

B

a coach to ask further questions in an attempt to arrive at a reason for a breakdown or lack of development in a particular ball skill. The failure of a player to select the right information from the display might be because he does not know what to look for, either because he has not had enough experience in the situation or because his attention has not been directed towards appropriate information in the display or *has* been directed towards inappropriate information. This stresses the importance once again of the coach being aware of information in the display which is worth having in relation to the performance of particular ball skills and at particular levels of skill development. Very often the coach restricts his comments to 'watch the ball'! Limitations in this respect are reviewed in the next chapter.

Putting the wrong interpretation on information which has been received may again reflect inexperience in a particular situation or a lack of awareness of possibilities. In as far as the art of misleading the opposition in a ball-game is considered to be an essential part of competitive play, players are in fact concerned with confusing the display (by for example dummying, feinting, changes in tactics, etc.) in such a way that opposition players either put a wrong interpretation on selected information or selectively attend to less important cues. This procedure might be considered in some instances as an additional social skill to be acquired, since control of the ball itself in such situations may be incidental. Other possibilities of this nature can be exploited by the interested reader.

At an everyday level, considerations such as those outlined above may lead to an adjustment in training techniques based on the appropriate monitoring of skill deficiencies rather than on vague ideas of where such difficulties might have arisen.

Categories of Ball Skills

Three general categories of task in the performance of ball skills can be outlined:

1. The acquisition* of a ball in flight via the visual pathway followed by capturing it in the hand(s) or into an instrumental extension of the hand(s) such as a lacrosse stick.

---

* In this context refers to focussing the eye(s) on the ball in flight and tracking it through all or part of its trajectory.

2. The acquisition of a ball as in category 1 followed immediately or after a minimal period of time by its direction towards a target which might be stationary or moving (as in batting skills or throwing in from the field at rounders).

3. Propelling an already acquired ball towards a target (as in golf, or a stationary corner kick in football).

A descriptive model for skills in categories 1 and 2 is given in Figure 5.

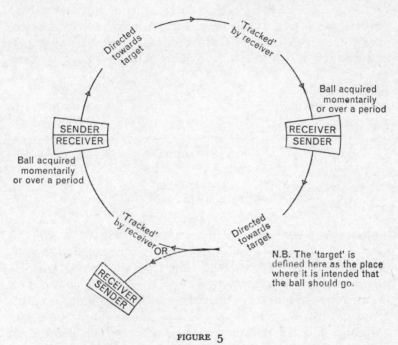

FIGURE 5

A simple model for ball skills in categories 1 and 2

'Open' and 'Closed' Skills*

Knapp (1964) extrapolating from the work of Poulton (1957) has classified skills in categories 1 and 2 as being towards the 'open' end of an open-closed skill continuum while skills coming under category 3 would be towards the 'closed' end. Basically, the continuum (Figure 6) ranges from skills which are pre-

---

* By 'closed' is implied that sensory feedback which guides the skill is in terms of proprioception while in 'open' skills, information for guiding the skill comes primarily from the display.

dominantly habitual (closed) through to skills which are predominantly perceptual (open). In the former:

> . . . conformity to a prescribed standard sequence of motor acts is all important

and in the latter

> at every instant the motor activity must be regulated by and appropriate to the external situation.

While on a broad basis, a general classification of this nature serves a useful purpose in emphasising the relative characteristics of these categories of skills, a too literal interpretation can be misleading. For example, in many of the ball skills in which

Skills which are predominantly habitual		Skills which are predominantly perceptual
'closed'	'closed-open'	'open'

FIGURE 6
Skill Continuum

interest here lies, the ball is hit with a *ballistic* movement of the hand or instrumental extension of the hand. Such movements, because of their relatively short duration and speed are pre-programmed in the central mechanisms as a 'whole' and cannot be influenced by current information monitoring (Vince, 1948b). However, the decision as to when to initiate the appropriate ballistic action is based on the monitoring of 'ball flight' and, depending upon the game, positions of other players. Thus, a primarily (*N.B.*) perceptual skill (*when* to do it) subserves a primarily motor ballistic action (*what* to do). It would appear that sports skills classified as being toward the 'open' end of the continuum may in fact be made up of skills which are mainly guided by external feedback as well as those mainly guided by internal feedback. Such skills might be described as 'closed' skills in an 'open' situation.

Skills included under categories 1 and 2 lay great emphasis on the acquisition of the ball in a situation in which the changing nature of the display is of great importance. For this reason alone, it may be considered that sports skills as such are relatively complex. Indeed, as Poulton (1965) has suggested, in hitting a moving ball three reasonably precise predictions are necessary:

1. The correct stroke to use—which may or may not be a ballistic action.

2. Where to pass the ball after it has been acquired.

3. Correct timing in order to hit the ball with the right amount of power when it is in the correct place. This involves predicting when the ball will be in the correct place for hitting, when to initiate the stroke to reach the ball at that time and the effort to be applied to the stroke.

All this information may be computed in a fraction of a second and adaptive responses carried out. Those who underestimate the magnitude of this feat on the part of the human brain should consider with the late Paul Fitts (1964) the difficulties involved in programming a computer to hit a base-ball bowled by a top-class pitcher!

There are of course implications here for the skilled player who has the difficult task of teaching his particular game to a beginner. Many coaches and teachers will be in this sort of position at one time or another. They may not appreciate the difficulty involved at the level of their students as they may no longer be aware of the stages through which their skill has developed in progressing from the novice to the competent performer stage. Successive chapters attempt to clarify some of the basic issues involved, in an attempt to get the teacher of ball skills to base his instruction on a knowledge of those principles which are fundamental to an understanding of the acquisition of such skills.

CHAPTER 2

Input Characteristics

Traditionally, it has been assumed that 'keeping the eye on the ball' is essential to the efficient performance of ball skills. Writers of textbooks on the teaching of games in which a ball is involved seldom make any explicit differentiation in this respect between beginners at the skill or competent performers. This premise has become so basic, even in those relatively easy skills such as hitting a stationary ball, that it seems unlikely that such instruction based on a wealth of practical experience should be entirely without foundation. However, it is part of the purpose of this book to question accepted procedures in the acquisition of ball skills and to review their implications in terms of experimental findings. That which has always been done or accepted is not necessarily right and may even be wrongly interpreted. Take for example the question of whether the left arm is straight in the golf swing or whether a fast hand action is necessary in the impact zone. Comparatively recent photography had answered 'no' to the first question and 'yes' to the second. Only when really sophisticated camera techniques were used late in 1967 (Dobereiner, 1967) was the fallacy of these 'accepted' interpretations brought into question (Plates 3 to 6).

The general trend of instruction in relation to the eye on the ball is exemplified by Rangecroft (1961) in discussing the acquisition of badminton skills:

The fundamental principle of keeping your eye on the shuttle always applies. . . .

and by Bradman (1958) in his text on cricket:

. . . try to glue the eyes on the ball until the very moment it hits the bat. This cannot always be achieved in practice but try.

However, when it is a case of trying to make a catch there is no exception whatever to the rule—watch the ball all the way.

Similar directions are given by writers in the sports of basketball (Meissner & Meyers, 1950), cricket (Townsend, 1953; McCool, 1961; Warner, 1941), squash (Morgan, 1953; Pawle, 1951) and tennis (Moss, 1956; Mottram, 1966; Fraser, 1962) to quote but a small sample taken at random. Hubbard & Seng (1954) quote similar examples from the American literature on baseball (Barber & La Mar, 1930; Bolin, 1950; Chapman & Severeid, 1941 and Jessee, 1939).

The general concensus of opinion appears to be that the ball is the primary consideration as far as visual attention is concerned and little emphasis is placed on the changeover from 'ball' to 'target' (in this instance defined as the place where the ball is intended to go after acquisition) either during the process of acquiring the ball or afterwards. At the same time, it would appear that looking at the target is not altogether incidental. Thus, Hankinson (1951) in relation to the tennis serve instructs:

Left shoulder pointing to the target and eyes on the target. . . .

It is not clear as to when this instruction applies because there is some stage in tennis serving at which visual attention needs to be focussed on the ball. The important consideration here —and in all ball skills—would seem to be:

1. Why do players need to look at the ball?

2. How long does visual attention need to be on the ball in a particular skill?

3. At what stage(s) in the performance of a skill does attention need to be on the ball?

4. At what stage(s) in the performance of a ball skill should attention be directed from the ball to a target or other part of the display?

Perhaps of even greater importance, is the question of how particular situations and stages of learning influence these four considerations. Unequivocal answers to these questions are not available at the present time. In addition, the wide variations in situations and range of possible ball skills would preclude the presentation of standard answers. There are however general findings from the field of experimental psychology which throw some light on these problems.

It is possible that writers of textbooks on ball games are placing emphasis on techniques necessary only for the beginner. If this is so, it is seldom made explicit and certainly in many cases there appears to be extrapolation from what expert players are *presumed* to do, to what is necessary for the beginner. A further source of confusion may be that the expert and the beginner are watching the ball for different reasons. The changing nature of task requirement as skill develops, has recently been elaborated by Fleishman & Rich (1963) in their investigation into the role of kinaesthetic and spatial-visual ability in perceptual motor skill learning.*

Although the generality of instruction to watch the ball all the time pervades the literature, there are hints that some writers are aware of both the difficulty and utility of doing so. Thus, Moss (1956) in discussing the problem of watching the ball on to the racquet in tennis states:

> It is extremely doubtful whether this is really possible, but it will be found when watching the ball really carefully that just before the moment of impact one sees the ball with an 'awareness' that the racquet is just on the point of striking it.

Here, the writer would appear to be questioning the physical possibility of watching the ball on to the racquet rather than an *intention* to do so.   This may also suggest why some experts say that they do watch the ball on to their bat or racquet—the *intention* to do so is confused with what actually happens.   Such an interpretation follows the Gestalt psychologists' principle of 'closure' (Osgood 1964) discussed in the game situation by Hubbard & Seng as follows:

> . . . accurate prediction of the ball's path and sensory cues from the bat contact might be merged to form an illusion of seeing the ball 'hit' and knowing where it should go . . . human perception customarily bridges gaps in sensory information and merges stimuli from diverse modalities to a unitary impression.

Information Processing

If it is so important to watch the ball all or some of the time, why is this so?   Generally speaking, the intention would appear

* See also Chapter 7.

to be to obtain information about the characteristics of the flight of the ball with a view to initiating the appropriate response—an aspect of selective learning (Noble, 1966).

Morgan (1953) in her book on the playing of squash racquets reflects the opinion of many other coaches when she stresses the need to know at what speed the ball is travelling and to know exactly where the ball has been hit. In this respect she is stressing the need for information about the *position* and *velocity* of the ball. Moss (1956) has also pointed out that the object of watching the ball throughout its flight and particularly after it bounces, is to be able to judge its pace, direction and height and to act or react according to the interpretation of the visual cues obtained. Once again, a consideration of position and velocity with the addition of direction. It would appear therefore that the eyes are being used to obtain information which will enable a player to *anticipate* both spatially and temporally future behaviour of the ball prior to its accurate interception by a limb or instrumental extension thereof. Neither of the above writers deal with a third factor about which information would seem to be important. It will be appreciated that a ball in flight is unlikely to be travelling at a constant velocity for any period of time. In order to make prediction more precise, knowledge of the rate of change of velocity—acceleration/deceleration—would also be necessary. Such terminology is in keeping with a model of the control characteristics of human movement in servomechanism terms.

The analogy between servomechanisms in engineering and human performance has been suggested by the stability attained by the neuromuscular system under diverse circumstances. This is accomplished by the use of some form of 'error-sensing' device which tests the difference between a desired movement and what has already been achieved (Ruch, 1951). Such error correction is brought about by the use of feedback circuits such as have already been described (page 6).

In the present context, the eyes operate as an error-sensing device providing feedback in terms of position, direction, velocity and acceleration (probably based on the rate of change in apparent size of the ball) on which information the player can make his future behaviour adaptive. It will be appreciated from Figure 7 that in ball skills where the ball approaches directly at the player (or nearly so), the angle subtended by the ball at the eye will change at a rate depending upon the speed of the ball. This is not the only information utilised in assessing velocity and acceleration. Apparently, the estimate of such characteristics may also be affected by the relationship of the moving object to its background (Vernon, 1965). Differences might also be expected when the ball is silhouetted against a relatively homogeneous background (the sky or a sight-screen in cricket are good examples) as compared with when it moves across a variegated background. In the former case its velocity will appear to be less than in the latter (Brown, 1931).

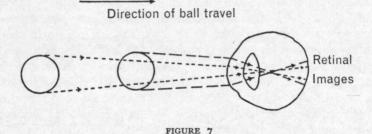

Direction of ball travel

FIGURE 7

Changes in the angle subtended at the eye by the ball and changes in the retinal image size as the ball approaches the eye directly

Although positional cues may be useful in orientating a player's attention, difficulties are imposed on the usefulness of such information by the time lag inherent in the nervous system in the processing of information. Thus, by the time *positional* information about a ball in flight has been fed back and processed, the ball will normally have changed position. An early paper by Gibbs (1954)—which still merits attention—on servo-principles in skill, anticipated much of the current work in this area. He points the disadvantages in feedback systems as follows:

> The time lags in the nervous system are long and a derivative term is therefore required in the feedback from a moving limb in order to avoid instability, and it is also required to give the familiar phenomenon of anticipation. Anticipation is essentially a process of extrapolating from current sense data to some future physical state and as such continuous data are required on the rate of change of state.

It is not difficult to understand how beginners at a ball skill will not be able to deal with all the information which is available to them until they have been in the situation long enough to detect the characteristics (position, velocity, etc., of the ball) of the system in which they are operating (Craik, 1947). Their initial focus of attention may be purely on positional information and mistakes will obviously follow. With very young children and others who have little experience in ball skills, considerable practice is necessary in order to appreciate even the elementary principles of anticipation. It might be that skill increases when higher derivative information is monitored or increase in skill may lead to the monitoring of higher derivative information. It is more likely that there is a reciprocal relationship between the two processes. Such a procedure has been well elaborated by Garvey & Mitnick (1957) in their description of the servo-system approach to perceptual-motor skill development in a tracking skill. These workers suggest that the human control system behaves progressively with training as a more complicated servomechanism. Initial error in the display is based on *positional* and *velocity* characteristics of the input data, but later in training, error *acceleration* and $\triangle$ *acceleration* (jerk) are the major influences in control. A procedure of this nature has been referred to by Fitts, Bahrick, Noble & Briggs (1961) as the 'progression hypothesis'. Support for such a model of perceptual-motor skill learning has been more recently provided by Fuchs (1962) in elaborating what he terms the 'progression-regression' hypothesis. This work indicated that under unfavourable conditions—such as stress—the performer reverts to an earlier level of control and his skill suffers accordingly. In view of what is known about the effects of stress on skilled performance, this hypothesis might well bear closer examination in a ball-skill context.

Predicting Ball Flight (Plates 7 and 8)

In the kind of visual motor coordination involved in ball skills, attention is clearly being drawn to the need to obtain visual information and the implication is that this can only be done by watching the ball *all* the time. That such an implication may be a fallacy is suggested by Kay (1957) in discussing the flight of the ball in a games situation:

We may compare this situation with the case of someone trying to estimate the future position of a moving object say a car or the trajectory of a ball from a limited observation of its initial stages. If we throw a ball for a young child to catch he is invariably too late in positioning his hands and lets the ball hit him on the chest. We say he doesn't anticipate the flight of the ball; he doesn't know where it will go but only where it is. Let us imagine the situation is such that our adult subject's head is fixed and he can only observe the trajectory of the ball by successive fixations. Thus we have the trajectory divided into a series of segments which one might think of as events, a, b, c and so on. An individual through his experience of watching how objects travel in space learns about the probable order and temporal relations of these events. Thus, given events a, b, c he predicts the future position: and the skilled person is the one who can predict accurately on the fewest possible initial events. Once this is achieved the remaining events in the series are redundant or at the most confirmatory. So much for the popular dictum about 'keeping your eye on the ball?!

Three points are particularly worth noting in Kay's statement:

1. He is dealing with a ball travelling on a predictable path. That is to say the observer in question 'knows' the trajectory of the ball on the basis of previous experience.

2. The observer 'knows' the trajectory of the ball because he has had the opportunity to learn the sequential dependencies (what follows what) of appropriate ball cues (position, velocity, acceleration and direction).

3. Looking at the ball although not being *necessary* from the point of view of taking in information may be *useful* in a confirmatory way, i.e. may confirm what the player has already predicted and thus be reassuring to him (particularly if he is unsure of his predictions) or may confirm in the sense of showing that the ball has not in fact deviated from its flight path.

There is another consideration which will need to be raised later in the chapter. While it may be possible to predict the trajectory of a ball from early cues, it must be asked how accurately such a prediction can be carried out. In many ball skills, exactness is not necessarily crucial since there is a reasonable range of 'error' within which to work.

There is presumably nothing which is innate in a person's

understanding of the parabolic flight of a ball.   Because it may
be possible to fit a mathematical equation to a flight path, it does
not mean that a player does not have to experience situations in
practice before he can be capable of making accurate predictions.   It might however suggest that knowledge of the
mechanical principles underlying ball flight would be a useful
training device.   Advantages might also be obtained by giving
very young children experience of a large number of different
ball flight situations since knowledge about flight characteristics
of a ball are acquired over a period through a player's interaction with many different ball situations.

While some transfer of training from one ball game to
another might be anticipated on the basis of common principles
of ball flight, it is also necessary to realise that the behaviour of
the ball in some games or game situations may be relatively
specific.   This may be more particularly true for those games
where spin, chop, hang, swing or bias are given to the ball and
where playing surfaces may give rise to ball movement which
could not be predicted.   For these reasons, it is questionable
whether in many ball games the ball is ever on a completely
predictable path except to the player who has experienced so
many different playing situations in that sport that he is able to
select the appropriate cues for response even in such difficult
circumstances.   It may be on this basis alone that the beginner
in a ball skill situation does need to watch the ball virtually all
the time.   Nevertheless, it does seem possible that players can
learn the relative prediction of even complex ball flights and in
many cases as will be illustrated later, come to make their
predictions from very early cues and at times almost before the
ball has left their opponent's area.   The situation would appear
to differ as between relatively slow ball games and slower
aspects of particular fast ball games (e.g. spin bowlers in cricket,
defensive players in table-tennis, etc.).   Clearly from the point
of view of 'acting upon information received' it is not possible
to watch the ball all the time in a fast ball skill—the need to
react and the resultant reaction time and movement time are
limiting factors which will receive attention in Chapter 3.

Experimental Findings
The discussion in this chapter so far has centred mainly
around theoretical concepts.   While these are useful and serve

to stress the problems that exist and possible solutions, it would be informative to have the results of experimental work in this area.   Unfortunately, there is an almost complete absence of experimental literature in the field of ball skills.   In view of the large number of people participating in such sports, this lack is to say the least surprising.   But, perhaps not so surprising when it is recalled that until comparatively recent years coaches in these games received little training in scientific techniques so that coaching could and still can to a large extent be called an art rather than an applied science.   It must of course be admitted that at the present time the art is a sophisticated one but scarcely lends itself to the exposing of myths which may have been handed down from coach to player through the generations.

One of the major difficulties in carrying out investigations into ball skills—particularly those concerned with eye movements and visual monitoring—is the inherent difficulty of recording results.   To a large extent, the experimenter is limited either to photographic methods in actual playing situations (which can lead to misinterpretations such as were illustrated earlier in the chapter) or to laboratory-type methods in which opportunity for viewing the ball in flight is restricted and the subsequent effect on skilled performance recorded. Attempts at direct measurement of eye movements in other skill areas have been carried out for a number of years and the difficulties (outlined by Mackworth & Mackworth, 1958) slowly overcome.   Four standard methods of recording eye movement data have been reported by Ford, White & Lichtenstein (1959).   Most of the original work on eye movements was related to primarily perceptual skills—the difficulty from the point of view of gross physical skills being the limitations and size of the early recording apparatus.   More recent developments by Mackworth and by Shackel (1960) have led to the design of portable apparatus incorporating cine or television cameras.

A further difficulty to be expected and resolved in interpreting the data obtained from eye movement recording is the difference between 'looking' and 'seeing', i.e. between orientation and perception.   There is no surety that because for example a person looks towards a ball that he is in fact seeing it—in terms of taking in information.   This applies equally well to actual situations as well as those in the laboratory and may well account for some of the interpretations put on procedures like keeping the eye on the ball. Adams (1966) puts the point succinctly as follows:

> Because of these various differences between looking and seeing—between being merely orientated to a stimulus and discriminating it—I think that we must throw our weight in the direction of seeing or, more generally, the observing response, which not only implies receptor orientation but also stimulus reception and discrimination for the criterion response that follows. . . . Measurements of eye movements and looking should not be totally discounted and set aside however. Measurement of eye movements can be worthy for no other reason than that motor behaviour and eye movements have not been studied jointly, and such research may bear far more fruits than my remarks here have indicated.

In addition to considerations of this nature, the early conditioning which has taken place within a ball-playing culture may make it difficult to find subjects who will not automatically keep their eyes on the ball in any experimental situation. Again, they may be 'looking' from habit without actually 'seeing'!

In a study already referred to (page 13) Hubbard & Seng (1954) used photographic techniques in a study of visual movements of baseball batters. Although there are no difficulties with a bouncing ball in baseball, there is always the possibility of the ball dipping or swerving in the air. According to these writers, the batter playing a pitched ball has to contend with two main problems:

1. A sensory perceptual problem consisting of tracking a ball in flight that is moving directly towards the player and hence increasing in apparent size and on this information predicting whether or not to swing and if so where and when to initiate the swing.

2. The motor response problem involving the translation of the perceptual monitoring of ball flight into the appropriately graded batting response.

Hubbard & Seng questioned whether it was possible to visually track a fast moving ball up to the point of contact and whether tracking served any useful purpose in enabling contact between bat and ball to be made. Amongst their data, they included photographer's records of twenty-nine professional baseball players in practice sessions in order to examine variation of head and/or eye movements in batting. At the same time, they also examined the step and the swing. From an analysis of the film records they were able to conclude that eye movements were mainly used in the tracking of the ball when a swing was made (as opposed to following the ball past the plate). These eye movements did not appear to continue up to the point of contact suggesting that either the tracking was discontinued at a point beyond which it was unnecessary, or that it was impossible to track the very fast ball near the plate, or both. In addition, the eyes appeared to exhibit smooth tracking responses rather than saccadic movements (quick jumps from one fixation point to another).

No evidence was found of the eyes being focussed on the ball at the moment of contact but some of the skilled batters stated that they saw the bat contact the ball, inferring that all pitched balls could be tracked to contact by batters with superior visual acuity and that failure to do so was due to defective vision or form. Hubbard & Seng conceded that this might be the case and that there might be special circumstances under which all balls could be tracked to contact on certain 'pitches'. However, they were also aware of the possibility of 'closure' (page 14) on the part of the players.

A further interesting finding in relation to the coordination of perceptual information and motor response was that the start of the step was geared to the release of the ball by the pitcher. The ball speed dictated the duration of the step and the start of the swing. The start of the swing and the end of the step tended to be coordinated by the swing starting about 0·04 secs. after the placing of the foot on the ground. The swing tended to take the same time whatever the speed of the ball.

Whiting (1967) in an ongoing series of experiments concerned with relating the effect of varying the direction of visual attention on performance in ball skills used laboratory-type apparatus in which opportunity for watching the ball in flight could be restricted. The skill selected for the initial experimentation was a continuous ball-throwing and catching task which would come into category 2 of those outlined in Chapter 1

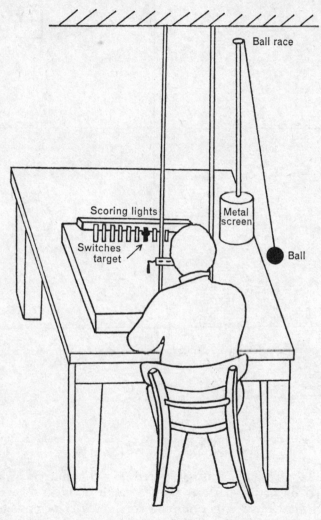

FIGURE 8

Modified table-skittles apparatus. *Whiting, 1967*

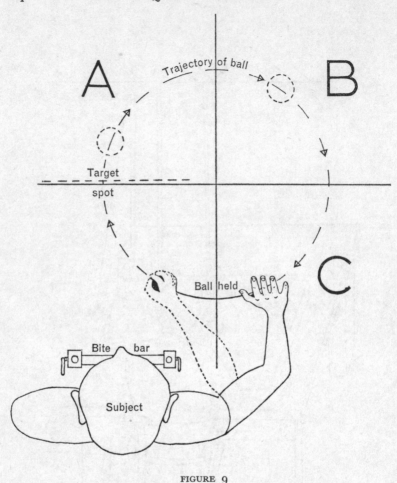

FIGURE 9

Plan of apparatus table showing quadrants in which ball could be illuminated (i.e., A, B, C). *Whiting, 1968*

(page 8). The apparatus devised for the purpose was a
modification of the parlour skittles game peculiar to certain
areas of the United Kingdom and commonly known as 'devil-
among-the-tailors'. Replacement of the traditional skittles by
electrical scoring switches (Figure 8) and modifications to the
pole around which the ball is swung enabled the ball to be lit
in various quadrants of its flight by a light within a metal
screen while remaining in darkness for the remainder of its
trajectory (Figure 9).

In the first experiment, players were trained for a period in full-light so that they could watch the ball during all of its trajectory. This was followed by requiring the players to perform the same task under a series of restricted light conditions including total darkness. Results of this experiment indicated that once having had the opportunity to watch the ball throughout the whole of its flight during a period of initial learning of the skill, it was possible to maintain performance at a similar level when opportunity for looking at the ball was restricted. The exception to this was the total darkness condition which showed a significant fall-off in performance when compared with the other restricted light conditions. It is worth noting that even in the dark, performance was reasonably good!

Observations on this 'pilot' experiment suggested the possibility of examining the effect of training subjects under restricted viewing conditions of the ball in order to discover the effect this might have on performance when such restrictions were removed (Whiting, 1968a). The rationale behind this approach was based on the possibility that although watching the ball all or most of the time was a normal procedure for the beginner at a particular ball skill, it was not a *necessary* procedure for the more experienced person. It is always tempting in devising training schedules to by-pass behaviour which appears only in early learning trials by training players on behavioural procedures utilised by the skilled performer.

For this experiment, a modification was made to the previous apparatus in the form of a pin-point of light which could be used to illuminate the target switch. The possible areas of illumination of the ball/target are again illustrated in Figure 9. These together with a full-light, a complete darkness and a target-only illuminated condition enabled seven possible variations to be considered. The results of this experiment are illustrated graphically in Figure 10 where the 'total score' represents a product of the number of throws and the accuracy achieved during one-minute sessions. The steady increase in performance by the players training under the full-light condition was to be expected as was the early decrease in scores under the restricted light conditions. There was obviously a need to readjust to the demands of the new restricted viewing conditions particularly with regard to catching the ball. The

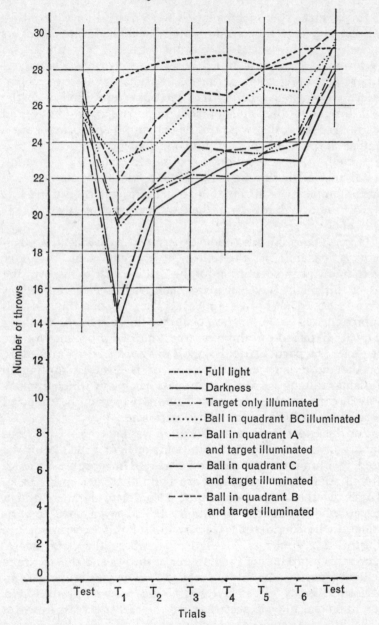

FIGURE 10

Results of training players under full light and restricted light conditions.
Whiting, 1968

decrease under restricted light conditions was only a temporary depression of performance and might reflect changes in tactical approach to the task. Within the space of six one-minute training sessions, subjects performing under conditions in which the target was illuminated and the ball in quadrants B or BC were not significantly different from those of the players training in full-light. Clearly, in *this* ball skill it is not necessary to watch the ball all the time in order to achieve a performance standard equivalent to that of a person who has always had the opportunity of observing the ball throughout the whole of its flight. As far as the present skill is concerned, there would appear to be an advantage in *particular* restricted light conditions. It is tempting to suggest that the player after releasing the ball is concerned with monitoring information about the score achieved rather than with watching the ball. This has probably been done by the time the ball reaches quadrant B when he can transfer his direction of vision from the scoring lights to the ball. Viewing the ball as it enters quadrant C would serve little purpose since by that time the catching response would be initiated and the incoming information would be at the most confirmatory. Such an interpretation is however speculative.

As a follow-up experiment it was considered worth while to discover what subjects actually do in a similar task situation when allowed reasonable freedom to develop their skill (Whiting, 1969). Since leaving the subject with complete freedom in the apparatus situation did not seem feasible as the uncontrolled variables would mask the information in which interest lay, an alternative procedure was adopted. The subject had the choice of looking at the ball or target but not both at the same time since it was arranged that only one of these light sources would be able to be switched on by the player at any particular time. In addition to the measure of the total score, information was monitored by the experimenter about:

a. the time for which the ball was held

b. the time the ball was in flight

c. the time for which the ball or the target were lit

d. the time before the ball was caught that the ball light was put out (i.e. target light put on).

The apparatus was again modified by removing the pole around which the ball had previously rotated and attaching the end of the supporting cord directly to a swivel in the ceiling. The wooden ball was replaced by a perspex ball which incorporated a bulb by which the ball could be illuminated. The upper hemisphere of the ball was coated with metal foil from which an electrical lead was connected to the recording apparatus. Subjects were trained over a period of ten sessions with a maximum of two days between each session and each session comprising five one-minute training trials. Results are shown graphically in Figure 11. It will be noted that a decrease in the amount of time for which the ball was lit occurred from trial to trial (except trials 2, 3 and 4 where it remained constant). These changes are reflected mainly in the amount of time before the ball is caught that the ball light is extinguished. The latter data is reflected in the curve at the bottom of Figure 11 (opposite). It will be noted that the ball-light is extinguished earlier and earlier before the ball reaches the player's hand,* that is to say, the ball is not being watched right into the player's hand after ten training sessions. These performance curves represent general trends within which there are considerable individual differences. Some players right from the initial trial did not watch the ball into their hand, others kept a more or less standard time for switching off the ball light before it reached their hand. Three widely differing curves for individual subjects are shown in Figure 12 (p. 30).

These experiments mark the beginning of attempts to solve some of the problems related to the acquisition of ball skills. But, it must be reiterated only a beginning and within a limited ball skill area. In the skills described in the above experiments the ball was *propelled* and caught by the same person—a situation which seldom exists in ball games unless the player is 'knocking-up' by himself. Thus, the player has '*outflow*' information available to him about for example the speed and direction in which the ball is being propelled.

Perceptual Units

To obtain information about the velocity or acceleration of a

---

* The shape of the curve should be noted rather than the measure in seconds given on the axis of the graph. The latter measurement includes the subject's reaction time and thus spuriously suggests that the ball is watched for longer than is actually the case. It is likely that all times should be adjusted by adding on approximately 0·18 secs.

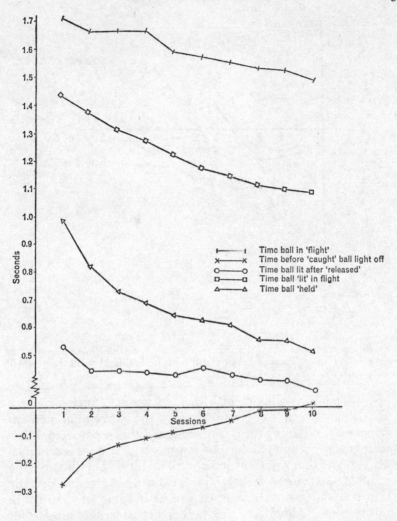

FIGURE 11

Performance curves for the combined means of all subjects. *Whiting, 1963*

ball it is necessary to view the ball while it is moving over a certain distance. It seems that information from a display is not processed continuously, but that information is taken in during brief periods and action (of the eye muscles or other effectors) is initiated as a result of the processing of 'chunks' of information (Broadbent, 1956). The implication here, is that the brain processes information discontinuously in time each

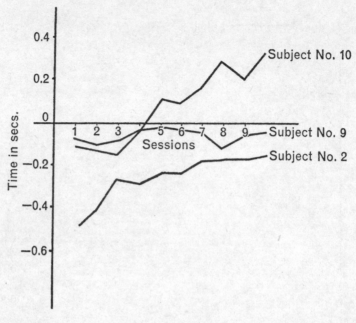

Performance curves of three subjects showing variations in the amount of time before the ball reached their hand that the ball-light was extinguished. *Whiting, 1969*

operation lasting a 'moment' (Shallice, 1964). Such a concept has been termed by Stroud (1955) the perceptual-moment hypothesis. White (1963) has suggested that a perceptual unit or moment occupies about 80–125 msecs. It does not necessarily follow that sufficient information will be obtained during a single moment. White (1967) has further suggested that the duration 250–300 msecs. appears to be in some way critical in this respect. Although there has been considerable support for such a hypothesis, it does not appear to have been tested within a ball-skill context.

Although the amount of time required to detect changes in the performance of a ball in flight are clearly important, it is also necessary to consider at what stage in the flight of the ball it is necessary for such perceptual moments to occur in order to make reliable predictions. Consider for example a ball dropping from a height of say 100′ under 'free fall' conditions. It would be on a predictable path but it is unlikely that viewing it say for a period of 250 msecs. at the very beginning of its flight would be sufficient to enable the ball to be caught, although it would probably give sufficient information to enable the catcher to get himself into roughly the right area to receive the ball. It is of course possible that a perceptual moment occurring very early and one occurring very late in the flight might give all the information that is required, but even here the initial one might be redundant. There is scope for a great deal of useful investigation in this area of skill performance.

With the above considerations in mind and with a view to making the laboratory situation more akin to that of a ball game, Whiting, Gill & Stephenson (1969) carried out an experiment on ball-catching in a situation in which the ball was caused to move on a parabolic flight path by mechanical means. A perspex ball ($2\frac{1}{2}''$ diameter) was used incorporating a bulb which enabled it to be illuminated over various parts of its trajectory in an otherwise blacked-out room. The ball-catching ability of 36 experienced ball players was assessed under the various restricted conditions adopted. The apparatus is illustrated in Figure 13 (overleaf). The ball was released from a height of 8′ by a mechanical release mechanism and fell vertically on to the miniature trampoline which caused it to enter on a parabolic flight path in the direction indicated in a similar way to that experienced in a number of ball games. When the ball hit the trampoline, it closed a switch (B) which activated an electronic circuit which caused the ball to light up during its flight for a length of time determined by a pre-arranged adjustment to the circuit. The total time of flight from the trampoline bed to the player's hand was 0·4 secs. The times selected for lighting up the ball were for periods of 0·1, 0·15, 0·20, 0·25, 0·30 secs. and full light from the moment that the switch at B was closed. The player's task was simply to catch the ball with one hand from a predetermined starting position. The results of this experiment are given in Figure 14.

The implications from these results are that catching ability improves as the time for which the ball is illuminated is increased suggesting that there is an advantage to be gained from watching the ball for as long as possible. These findings are important additions to those reported earlier by Whiting. It must, however, be remembered that in this particular experiment:

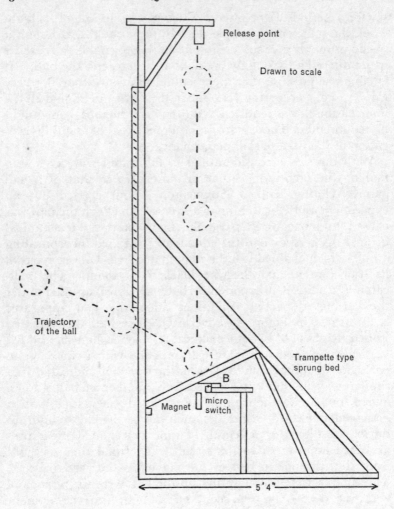

FIGURE 13
Ball-dropping gantry

a. all the subjects were competent performers before they started

b. the ball was on a relatively unpredictable path (restricted to some extent by requiring the ball to pass through a 15″ diameter hoop)

c. *outflow* information was not available since the player did not initiate the flight of the ball.

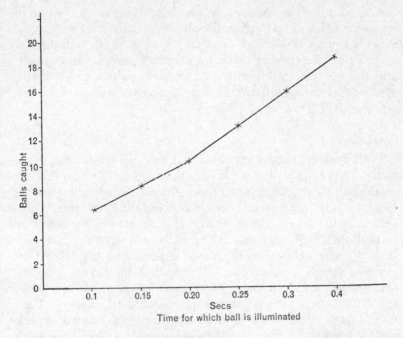

FIGURE 14
Number of balls caught (out of 20) under differing periods of illumination.
Whiting, Gill & Stephenson, 1969

It may be therefore that when the ball is on a relatively un-predictable path that it is necessary to take in more information on which to base predictions about its future position. This aspect will need to be looked at further.

It might be asked why there was a difference in the number of balls caught between the 0·3 secs. and the 0·4 secs. illumination conditions (particularly since such differences were significant). The difference of 0·1 secs. is less than a normal reaction time and it would be anticipated that monitoring of such information would have no effect on subsequent alterations to a movement which must have been initiated before such information was available. This difference can probably be accounted for by the performance of the subjects. Under the full-light con-dition, instead of coming forward with their hand to take the ball, they tended to give with the ball as it reached the region of their hand—as is done in catching in a normal game situation. In doing so, players will have artificially increased the amount of time from 0·4 secs. to something in the region of 0·5 secs. This did not occur for all players and it was apparent that those players who did not in fact 'give' with the ball showed very little difference in catching success between the 0·3 secs. and the 0·4 secs. conditions. As in the previous experiments, marked individual differences were apparent around the trend reported in Figure 14.

Conclusions

Both theoretical and experimental considerations lend some support to the idea that a player does not need to keep his eye on the ball for the whole of its trajectory *once he is familiar with the flight path* in particular situations. Learning is clearly involved in the latter statement and it is not surprising therefore to find that beginners watch the ball for longer periods than they do when they become more experienced and also that many of them will watch the ball right into their hand. Again, this would appear to differ even in experienced players when the ball is travelling on a less predictable trajectory. Care must however be taken in extrapolating from limited experimental findings. There is obviously a need to extend the work carried out to date.

Hubbard & Seng (1954) commenting on the fact that eye movements did not continue up to contact of bat with ball suggest that:

> . . . either the tracking was broken off at some point beyond which additional information would have been superfluous since the bat was on its way, or was broken off because the visual apparatus broke down—became incapable of tracking at the very high relative velocity of a pitched ball near the plate—or both.

Subjects in these baseball experiments were experienced players in a very fast ball game situation.

In general, it would seem that with beginners in any ball skill, it is important to encourage 'keeping the eye(s) on the ball' for fear that they take their eye(s) away too soon. It might be profitable to draw the attention of learner players to reasons for watching the ball and instruction in the mechanics of ball flight might be a useful technique. Although the beginner probably needs to watch the ball for as long as possible in order to take in the necessary visual information which will determine his actions, the expert is able to utilise information which comes at an early stage in ball flight. But even the expert may need to watch the ball longer when the ball is on a relatively unpredictable path. In addition, he may continue to keep his eye on the ball in order to stabilise his head position or to maintain his body in the most mechanically efficient position for catching or stroke production.

It is important to realise that the skill of catching or hitting a ball and the ability to pick out the early, vital cues in any display for the purpose of predicting future behaviour of the ball in a countless number of different situations may take many years to experience and perfect. Finally, the expert will not only need to watch the ball for less of its flight, but he will also require less time to discriminate, programme and make decisions on the information that he receives about position of the ball, direction and force of wind, state of the ground, position of other players and the many other cues in the display during any games situation. There are of course other limitations for even the experts and these will be discussed in the next chapter.

CHAPTER 3

Decision Making

Reaction time is one of the limiting factors in the performance of all skills. Although comparatively little work has been attempted on reaction time in relation to ball skills, a vast literature on the subject exists in the field of experimental psychology. Basically, reaction time can be considered under two categories:

1. Simple reaction time
2. Choice reaction time (dysjunctive reaction time)

both of which are worth considering in the present context.

Simple Reaction Time

Although definitions differ from writer to writer, it would generally be agreed with Teichner (1954) that simple reaction time is:

> . . . the interval between the onset of the stimulus and the initiation of the response under the condition that the subject has been instructed to respond as quickly as possible.

In general, it will be found that reaction times for a given individual will differ according to the sense modality through which stimulation for response is received. At the same time, it is reasonably clear that a person whose reaction time is fast to a stimulus through one sense modality will be comparatively fast to stimuli received through all other sense modalities and similarly a person whose reaction time is slow to a stimulus through one sense modality will be slow to stimuli received through all other sense modalities. Typical reaction times for various sense modalities are given in Figure 15 (Woodworth & Schlosberg, 1963). While in most ball games concern will be with reaction time to visual stimuli (often the ball), the contribution of other senses in this respect must not be ignored.

36

Stimulus	Reaction Time in Millisecs.
Light	180
Sound	140
Touch	140
Kinaesthesia*	146

(*Data for kinaesthesia taken from Wilkinson (1958). See also Vince (1948), Chernikoff & Taylor (1952), Denenberg (1953) and Slater-Hammel (1955)).

FIGURE 15

Variations in simple reaction time for different sense modalities

Although for example the sound of the ball hitting a wall or a bat, is apparent in most ball games, the possible utilisation of sound cues does not seem to have been investigated. If these do play a part in organising responses, it is worth noting the faster reaction to an auditory stimulus. It is also known that when stimulating two sense modalities simultaneously—such as by light and sound—the reaction will be to the stimulus which has the faster associated reaction time. Anecdotal evidence can be recounted from an actual game situation which may have a bearing on this topic. Repairs to a local squash court exterior wall resulted in the need for intermittent hammering on the wall. Two regular players on the court at the time had to cut short their game. They contended that the sound of the hammering on the wall was interfering with the monitoring of the sound of the squash ball resulting in a fall-off in performance.

The intensity of the stimulus can also influence reaction time (Woodworth & Schlosberg, 1963). Considerations of this nature may account for some of the difficulties encountered in playing games during bad light conditions or other distracting situations which make the discrimination of the ball from the background difficult.

Four main latencies contribute to the length of reaction time:

i. Sense organ time (e.g. time taken for chemical processes in the retinal cells of the eye). This would appear to account for some of the difference between visual and auditory reaction time.

ii. Decision time in the central mechanisms of the brain—accounting for most of the delay in reaction time.

iii. Nerve transmission time—relatively fast so that differences from individual to individual may not be significant.

iv. Muscle time—the delay between the impulse arriving at the motor end plate and the actual muscular response.

Providing that the subject is familiar with the apparatus situation being used to record reaction time, it would not appear to be amenable to training. A study by Gibson, Karpovich & Gollnick (1961) reported a shortening not only of reaction time but also of reflex time after a six-week training period. However, the absence of a control group in this study makes the results difficult to interpret. It would not be surprising if a period of training in a relatively untrained person resulted in changes in muscular latency leading to an apparent decrease in reaction time. (Times normally reported for latency of muscle vary between 20 and 30 milliseconds.)

It is important to distinguish reaction time from movement time. This is not difficult if it is remembered that reaction time is concerned with the moment of initiation of the response and not the *duration* of the response. There does not appear to be any simple relationship between reaction time and movement time (Poulton, 1965).

Having clarified some of the issues involved, it must now be stated that it is unlikely that simple reaction time as measured in the laboratory is analogous to any situation in ball games! Hubbard & Seng (1954) are particularly against such an interpretation when they state:

. . . batting is not primarily a reaction time problem. The stimulus object (ball) is continuously visible during its flight, and not suddenly presented. Consequently the problem is one of tracking a moving object, predicting its course and, at some point in its flight, deciding to swing or not. Thus, prediction subserves the motor response. Although generating momentum in the bat and the preceding central processes involve some duration, any sensory component in reaction time is essentially eliminated. In other words, estimates based on reaction time or when the batter must make his decision and start the process which will result in the swing, place the point too far back in terms of ball flight. . . . Following the specified rules for determining when the signal must

1. The display to a car-driver.

2. The display to a badmington player.

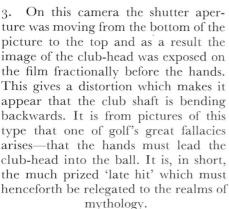

3.   On this camera the shutter aperture was moving from the bottom of the picture to the top and as a result the image of the club-head was exposed on the film fractionally before the hands. This gives a distortion which makes it appear that the club shaft is bending backwards. It is from pictures of this type that one of golf's great fallacies arises—that the hands must lead the club-head into the ball. It is, in short, the much prized 'late hit' which must henceforth be relegated to the realms of mythology.

4.   Here is exactly the same moment in time taken on a camera with the shutter aperture moving from top to bottom. In this case the hands were snapped before the club-head, which had time to advance several inches and almost make contact with the ball. Notice that the hand position in all the pictures is virtually the same. In this type of camera the distortion frequently suggests that the shaft is bending forward and from this photographic trick many teachers have deduced that extra zip is imparted to the ball by the whipping action of the shaft.

(Photographs by Chris. Smith, by courtesy of *The Observer*)

5. Probably the most accurate representation of the impact position, this picture was taken on a camera with the aperture moving from left to right. From this angle the shaft appears to be virtually straight (although in fact it is bowing slightly towards the camera). The club-head at this point is moving at something like 170 feet per sec. and the shutter, travelling in the same direction, has 'frozen' it in pretty much its real position. All these first three cameras were of the focal plane type, of modern design and popular today for sports photography.

6. This is the only picture taken with a camera having a compur shutter, which takes in the whole scene at once. At this speed (1/500 sec.) there is blurring in direct proportion to the speed of the different parts of the subject. Pictures of this kind give a cinematic effect, showing the relative movement of hands and club-head during the business part of the swing. The deduction which can be drawn is that talk of 'a fast hand action in the impact zone' is so much hog-wash. Power comes from the sweep of the club-head past the line of the arm.

(Photographs by Chris. Smith, by courtesy of *The Observer*)

7. Keep your eye on the ball?

8. Keep your eye on the ball?

9 & 10.   The difficulty experienced by a young child in catching a ball pitched
at about 15 m.p h. from a distance of 10′.

11 & 12.   Notice that the hands have not had time to move before the ball goes through and hits her on the chest.

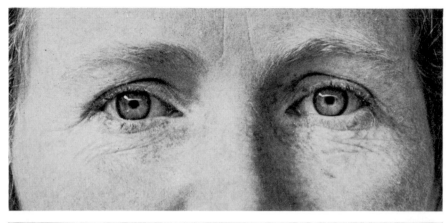

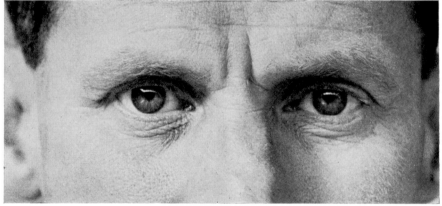

13 & 14.   Differences in inter-pupillary distances.

occur in assuming batting is a reaction time situation, we find
first, that only for very slow balls could the signal occur
inside the last half of ball flight; and second, that the batter
must be prepared to react and swing on the basis of some
signal which may occur before the pitcher releases the ball.
Since he cannot know until release by the pitcher what the
situation will be and since the first part of ball flight provides
very poor cues, how can he differentiate between even a fast
and slow ball, let alone estimate its direction? We found
that the batters did respond differently to balls at different
speeds. They responded differently to ball arriving in
different positions—by hitting them. Consequently, our
opinion that batting is a perceptual (and motor) problem
rather than something analogous to reaction time seems
valid.

Although Hubbard & Seng's comments seem to be very
relevant (in spite of the fact that the last sentence implies that
reaction time is something other than a perceptual and motor
problem!) they may be overstating their case. It is doubtful
whether a batter in cricket or baseball for example *can* differentiate between a fast and slow ball *if* the bowler conceals the
run-up or wind-up to either ball in such a way that the batsman
cannot perceptually distinguish it from other modes of delivery
and if the batsman is not aware of the possibility of such
an idiosyncrasy on the part of the bowler/pitcher. As was
indicated earlier (page 8) the whole art of deception in games
skills consists in either masking the visual display in such a way
that opponents misinterpret the cues or in presenting distracting
cues for response.

Further elaboration of this point can be made with reference
to the game of cricket and in particular the art of bowling.
The main attributes of the bowler are speed and/or guile. The
primarily fast bowler relies on speed alone to beat the batsman.
This type of bowling lends itself least to modification and it is
therefore more easy to learn to predict the flight path. The
slow bowler however, uses his guile in the manipulation of
length, flight and direction in an attempt to confuse the batsman. The batting situation therefore becomes one in which
the batsman has less time to play the fast ball which is more
predictable and more time to play the slow ball which is less
predictable! Two further factors in bowling which are worthy
of mention are 'spin' and 'cut' (that is deviation after the ball

D

has pitched) and swing (deviation in flight before pitching).
These are additional weapons in the bowler's armoury and on
his mastery of them will depend to a large measure, his success.
It is perhaps pertinent to point out at this stage that the last
bowler to take more than 200 wickets in an English County
cricket season was Lock in 1957 who was labelled as an unpredictable 'fast' bowler.   Another extremely successful bowler
was S. F. Barnes—a fast bowler with all the best attributes of a
slow bowler.   He could deliver away swingers, off-breaks, and
leg breaks all with sufficient velocity to make any batsman
hesitant:

> A typical over, first two very late outswingers straight enough
> and well enough up to force the batsman to play off the front
> foot, then two penetrating off-breaks, the fifth ball a fast
> leg-break and a leg-break it was rather than a leg cutter—
> and finally such a delivery as on his great Australian tour
> bowled Victor Trumper at the height of his powers, the ball
> swerving from the leg stump on to the off and then breaking
> back to hit the leg.   'It was the the sort of ball,' said Charlie
> Macartney, 'that a man might see when he was tight!' (Swan-
> ton, 1967.)

His achievements are worth quoting.   In the leagues his figures
were really in a class of their own.   He took 1,400 wickets at the
cost of less than eight runs each in county games and in league
games 3,700 for less than seven runs each.   He is the only bowler
to have averaged twelve wickets per match in a Test series.

The point being made by Hubbard & Seng in the quotation
given earlier, is that their batters did in fact hit balls which they
would not have been able to if accepted reaction time measures
were taken into account.   Unfortunately, this appears to be the
only available evidence in this respect.   A series of operational
analyses in different ball-game situations would throw light on
this neglected area of research.   The question which arises
here, is whether or not reaction time is faster to a stimulus which
is always present than to a stimulus which is presented/removed
in the typical laboratory situation?   In this connection, there *is*
experimental laboratory evidence in the form of what has been
termed *transit reaction time*.   This form of reaction time would
not appear to differ—in terms of times recorded—from the
measures of simple reaction time previously discussed (Belisle,
1963).   This statement must, however, be qualified, because

under conditions in which the stimulus is present *all* the time and is the focus of attention, expectancy is likely to be at its highest and hence the reaction time will be at its least (Mowrer, 1941). In addition, since the player is not having to wait for the sudden onset of a stimulus it might be expected that he would be able to concentrate on the organisation of the response. This in itself can result in a faster reaction time than if the concentration is on the stimulus (Lange, 1888).

Transit Reaction Time

. . . the task is to press a key, or make some such simple movement, at the instant when two objects approaching one another come into exact coincidence (Hick & Bates, 1948.)

Typically, experimental work in this area has involved stopping a revolving pointer exactly on a predetermined mark (for example stopping a stopwatch exactly on the zero mark). The response of pressing the button must be initiated one reaction time before the pointer reaches the mark in question (assuming that movement time is negligible). There is a difference in the ball-skill situation since a movement time is always involved. Thus, a player has to initiate his response one reaction time plus one movement time before the ball is in the position for hitting or catching. The difficulty of such predictions has already been discussed (page 17). Under such conditions, reaction time is going to be more critical in fast ball skills than those of a relatively more leisurely pace.

Although studies such as those of Knapp (1961), Slater-Hammel & Stumpner (1950) and Miller & Shay (1964) have drawn attention to the fast simple and choice reaction times of competent games players, the problem is more than that of fast reaction. As Poulton (1965) has pointed out:

Although reaction time is very much tied up with this kind of skill (fast ball skill) there is no simple relation between them. The man who is good at fast ball games, is not necessarily the man whose reaction time is the shortest when measured. The only certain generalisation is that the man with the long reaction time will not be good at fast ball games.

There is apparently a reasonable range over which the reaction time may vary without generally upsetting the skill.

A player can be very successful in a ball game without his timing being one hundred per cent perfect since there is usually a reasonable degree of 'error' possible without upsetting play too much. What it amounts to, is that the player with the faster reaction time can if he wishes let the ball travel further before initiating an action and theoretically at least he can use the additional time to monitor the other aspects of the display (particularly positions of other players). The player with the faster reaction time may if he wishes wait for later deviations in the flight of the ball and thus react more adaptively.

The possible limitations imposed by reaction time can be more easily demonstrated by reference to actual game situations:

(a) BASEBALL

Scott (1945) has shown that a fast overhand baseball throw requires from 0·43–0·58 secs. to travel from the pitcher to the home plate (60' 6") approx. Assuming that a transit reaction time to a visual stimulus was all that was involved (i.e. ignoring movement time), those players with the fastest reaction time would have to initiate their strike at the latest when the ball was still 20' away from the home base. Those with the slowest reaction time would be committed when the ball was about 30' away. Players with the fastest reaction time have an extra distance of 10' over which to view the ball and organise their responses.

It is unlikely that the movement time involved in making a strike would be less than the reaction time, so that some adjustment would have to be made to the above figures setting the initiation of the response further back in time.

(b) SOFTBALL

Miller & Shay (1964) in a study of the relationship of reaction time to the speed of a softball have shown that the ball travelling at approximately 60 m.p.h. takes 0·47 secs. from release to arrival at the home plate. The mean *laboratory* simple reaction time (*N.B.* not transit reaction time) to a visual stimulus for the 258 students used in the investigation was 0·215 secs. (range 0·156–0·370) to a visual stimulus. While the conclusion of these investigators about the impossibility of some of the players being able to hit the softball because of a slow reaction time must be questioned (since the players might react to cues from the pitcher's wind-up), they do draw attention to the very limited possibilities for players with a slow reaction time.

(c) CRICKET

Since no experimental work seems to have been done within the cricket situation, it is of interest to combine theoretical and practical laboratory findings in looking at limitations imposed by reaction time of the batsman in the game. Figure 16 gives the calculated flight path times at three fast ball speeds. In a laboratory study of reaction and movement times in cricket-type situation, Eastwood, Entwhistle, Gill & Stephenson (1968) were able to show a more or less constant *movement time* in a variety of situations in the region of 0·3 secs. The movement involved was stepping forward or backward in several directions as would be done in an actual playing situation. Assuming once again a reaction time to a visual stimulus to be in the region of 0·2 secs., it would seem that a time of about 0·5 secs. is necessary from the moment a decision is made to initiate a

Speed of Ball	Flight path (60′) time
80 m.p.h.	0·51 secs.
60 m.p.h.	0·68 secs.
40 m.p.h.	1·02 secs.

FIGURE 16

The relation of flight path time to the speed of the ball in a cricket situation

movement, to its completion. Reference once again to Figure 16 will indicate the limitations of watching the ball all the time in such a situation if the information from the ball is to be used in affecting the stroke. Even for a ball bowled at 10 m.p.h. the stroke will have to be initiated when the ball is approximately $7\frac{1}{2}'$ away!

The discussion so far has centred around the limitations imposed by reaction time on mature players. In as far as reaction time decreases on a maturational basis, it would be expected that even more limitations would be imposed on *children* in ball skill situations. Goodenough (1935) and Jones (1937) have shown the development in reaction time from the age of three years upward (Woodworth & Schlosberg, 1963)—Figure 17.

It will be noticed from this figure, that children at the age of five years have a reaction time which is almost double that of the adult. For a child of this age facing for example a ball thrown from a distance of 10' away, the limitations would be obvious. If the ball were thrown at only 15 m.p.h. and assuming there were no complications from movement time, the child would have to initiate his response as soon as the ball had left the thrower's hand! No wonder difficulties are encountered. There are of course additional complications in addition to reaction time limitations which further increase the difficulties (Plates 9 to 12).

Choice Reaction Time

Although many situations in ball games involve a transit reaction time, particularly when attention is primarily on the ball, there will be many other situations where the player will require to make a choice from amongst the many stimuli for response prior to carrying out an action. In addition to choice on the input side, there will also be situations in which a choice has to be made between a number of possible actions on the output side to one or more stimulus situations.

If a player is presented with *one* of a *set* of stimuli and a choice of response contingent on the stimulus is required, the corresponding time interval is known as the *choice reaction time*. Longer reaction times would normally be expected and are often apparent under such conditions when compared with the reaction time involved in making a single uniform response to a single uniform stimulus (simple or transit reaction time). Within any ball game, the particular response made will be determined not only by the flight characteristics of the ball, but by the positions of other players, the characteristics of the display and the strategy being adopted. A player—depending upon his degree of sophistication in the game—will have a repertoire of possible response patterns from which to choose. The player may have to differentiate between a variety of stimulus situations in the display and recognise the important cues for response from amongst the many conflicting cues which may be present. It has been suggested that the player learns what cues are worth attending to and what cues to be ignored as irrelevant. This is usually brought about by a combination of experience in different situations and good coaching. Thus, as the player becomes more experienced his choice of stimuli for attention become less as he realises what is important to particular situations within the game. It is likely that his choice of responses also becomes less as he realises

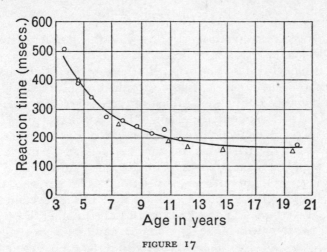

FIGURE 17

Changes in simple reaction time with age, from *Goodenough, 1935,* and *Jones, 1937. Woodworth & Schlosberg, 1963*

that a particular stroke/movement is more appropriate to particular cues from the display. There is however an anomaly here, because it is clear that really experienced players have a number of different ways of dealing with the same situation. They will be concerned again with masking the display by making their responses less predictable.

A better understanding of the principles being expounded above can be had from a consideration of some of the theoretical and experimental work on choice reaction time in the laboratory situation. Typically, in the laboratory choice reaction time experiment the subject will be faced with a stimulus panel comprising a number (which may be varied) of light sources corresponding to the number of stimuli which it is intended to use. In association with these stimuli will be a response panel containing for example microswitches activated by the subject's fingers which may or may not be compatible with the stimulus configuration (Figure 18). In such situations and with relatively naïve subjects (who have not practised on the apparatus but are familiar with its function) it has been found that choice reaction time (where the chances of any stimulus coming on are equiprobable) is proportional to the number of stimuli which are available for response (Hick, 1952). More specifically:

$$\text{Choice Reaction Time} = k \log (n + 1)$$

where k is a constant and n (2, 3, 4, 5, . . .) the number of stimuli from which the choice is made.

This model is based on what has been termed 'information theory' (Wiener, 1948). What is implied in this model is that the amount of information which any message (stimulus, cue, etc.) conveys is not only determined by that message itself, but is an increasing function of the number of possible messages from which the particular message *could* have been selected. For example it often happens in a ball game that the ball comes to a player from an unexpected position. The 'surprise' value of such a happening and hence the length of the reaction time will be determined to a large extent by the number of possible positions from which the ball might have been expected to come. In such situations, it is likely that the probability of the ball coming from particular positions may vary. An adapted formula from that given above is necessary if the stimuli presented are not equiprobable (Broadbent, 1965). Although the use of this model has been an incentive for much of the work in the area of reaction time, there has lately been considerable critique. While the model may well fit the situation described with naïve subjects, Laming (1962) draws attention to the failure of the model to deal with the effects of practice. Crossman (1955) also draws attention to the clear distinction which would seem to exist between the time for discrimination (or recognition) and the time for the selection of the response.

The latter critiques have arisen from the finding that with much practised subjects, the difference between choice reaction time to two or more signals does not differ. Experienced ball players will of course be very much practised! In addition, the greater the compatability between stimulus and response, the less the effect of varying the number of stimulus-response choices. This has been most clearly demonstrated by Leonard (1959) who showed that by giving stimuli direct to responding members (in this case the fingers) so that in effect no translation

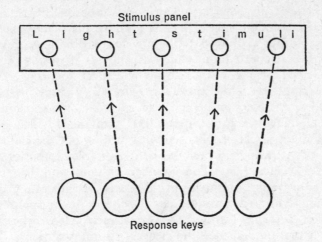

(a)   A compatible display

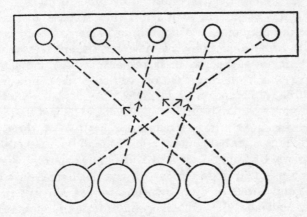

(b)   An incompatible display

FIGURE 18

The relationship between stimulus lights and response keys in what would be to an unpractised person:
  (a) a compatible display
  (b) an incompatible display

from sight to action is required, the relationship breaks down completely and responses are equally fast whatever the degree of choice.

It is now possible to return to the game situation and review it in relation to the laboratory findings.   A likely interpretation of the effects of practice and stimulus-response compatability on choice reaction time is that by practice the player learns to make stimulus and response more compatible! It must be realised that compatability in this sense is in terms of what experienced people would normally expect to occur. Even though displays such as those in Figure 18 (b) may be incompatible to a subject on his early trials, it is not surprising that with extended practice compatability is enhanced. In a games situation players are concerned with picking out the right cues for response whether these be ball cues, player positions or other characteristics. The number of cues and hence the number of choices on the input side decrease with practice and coaching. From a considerable array of possible responses in a situation, a player learns those responses which will best fit a given situation. Hence he learns stimulus-response compatability and behaves in accordance in a more adaptive way. As his experience develops and he becomes what is termed a sophisticated player, he will learn that it pays to make his responses unpredictable to opposition players. That is to say from the opposition point of view he attempts to make his response incompatible to their response which in fact is his stimulus! Such an incompatible response may, however, be compatible to the person performing.

The above position is further confused by the fact that players may be working up for particular strokes two or three stages ahead. This is probably more applicable to racquet games like table-tennis, badminton, squash and tennis where players may decide to use a strategy which will enable them to use a particular good stroke of their own on an occasion two or three exchanges ahead. It seems likely that they can in fact organise a series of general responses in advance although the exact nature of the stroke will be determined by the particular condition prevailing at the time. Thus for example a table-tennis player with a strong forehand drive might manipulate the play of his opponent over a series of predetermined strokes before finally getting him into position in which he can carry out the forehand 'kill'. The phenomenon of 'setting-up' an opponent occurs in this way in many games.

Psychological Refractoriness

It might be considered that watching the ball even after a

decision to begin the stroke had been made—would be useful from the point of view of stopping or changing the stroke if at a later stage the ball altered its path or if the stroke was deemed undesirable. But, within the short time intervals involved in ball skills, the 'psychological refractory period' would be a decidedly limiting factor. In slower ball skills or when hitting a stationary ball, continued watching of the ball might indeed serve such a purpose but ball skills in which such a relatively long interval of time between decision to strike and ball reaching striker must be relatively few. In a similar way ballistic strokes to a stationary or moving ball involve short time duration and must be considered to come into this category. Take for example experiments carried out on the golf swing (Noble, 1966). The golf swing is commonly thought of as consisting of two distinct parts—the backswing and the forward swing (or 'downswing').* Although it is difficult, in most cases to identify with certainty the precise time at which the one ends and the other begins (since the club, the arms and various parts of the body do not all reverse their direction at exactly the same time), the idea is quite a useful one. The backswing is the means whereby the player gets himself aligned and powerfully positioned for his forward swing; the latter is the positive all out swing at the ball.

The duration of the backswing can vary quite a lot from one player to another—from 0·6 secs. to 1·0 secs. but the forward swing, as might be expected, is more constant at around 0·2 secs. to 0·3 secs., part of that variation being merely a manifestation of the difficulty, already mentioned, of telling (from high-speed film, for example) when the forward swing actually begins.

One interesting point about this time interval is that it is typical of the time taken for the human neuro-muscular system to react to sensory information. The question therefore arises: to what extent is the golf swing a guided movement, and to what extent a ballistic one on which continuous control cannot be exercised?

Noble's method was to present each test golfer with a well-defined visual stimulus during his swing and to see how early it had to be applied before the swing was affected. This was done by having the golfers hit shots into a net in a room whose

---

* But see for example comments on bi-phasic movements—page 57.

only source of light could be switched off (with rapid decay) at various stages in the swing.

The subjects were not at first told the object of the experiment, and each one was allowed to hit five or six shots under the illusion that only clubhead speed was being measured. (It *was* being measured for comparison with later swings.) On the sixth or seventh swing, without warning, the light was switched off; on subsequent swings the subjects were told to continue hitting shots, but with the possibility that on any swing the light might go out, in which case they were to try to stop their swing. Comparison of the average clubhead speed over a portion of the swing, with the speed over the same portion in undisturbed swings was taken as an indication of how successful they had been in stopping their swings.

Results of these experiments indicated that:

(i) If the light went out just after the beginning of the downswing, 11 out of the 12 subjects could not alter their swing at all.

(ii) If the light went out just before the end of the backswing, all subjects could actually stop on *most* occasions.

(iii) However, those subjects, whose first 'surprise lights-out' occurred at this point in the backswing, did not stop on that single occasion.

(iv) The almost unanimous opinion of the subjects, when the light went out just after the beginning of the downswing, was that it had done so around the time of impact. Indeed some subjects thought that it was their striking the ball which had switched off the light!

The phrases, 'just after the beginning of the downswing', and 'just before the end of the backswing' were used rather than precise times, because the light was switched out by the interruption by the club of beams of light aimed across the plane of the swing at various places. Different golfers therefore broke these beams at slightly different times—though in general 'just after the beginning of the downswing' meant about 0·10 to 0·12 secs. before impact, and 'just before the end of the backswing' meant about 0·40 secs. before impact.

These results seem to confirm that no control which involves using sensory information can be exercised during the downswing—that the movement is, in fact, a ballistic one.

Further interesting information is also available from Noble's work. Although control *can* be exercised up to the end of the backswing, in normal circumstances *is* it? Or is it normally unnecessary to use any sensory information beyond an even earlier point in the swing?

In terms of the 'lights-out' experiment, if the subjects are told to try to continue the swing normally whatever happens, how *early* can the light be switched off without affecting the swing? (This, of course, will answer the previous question only so far as *visual* information goes.)

Noble tried this experiment and his provisional conclusions were that:

(i) The subject could swing normally and strike the ball accurately if the light remained on for only a few inches of his backswing.

(ii) Few subjects could strike the ball accurately, or even at all, if the light went out before the backswing began.

He concluded that, in addition to the downswing being ballistic, the whole golf swing is to some extent a 'programmed' event, in which visual information, at least, is unnecessary beyond quite an early stage. The same may not be true of information received via the proprioceptors, but it is a plausible hypothesis to say that successful golfers are those who succeed in programming their swings in such a way that no interruption or correction is needed.

The inability of golfers to stop their swing when the light went out just after the beginning of the downswing (about 0·11 secs. before impact) in the first experiment can probably be accounted for by the reaction time involved in initiating a new action. This in itself with the short time interval involved would be a sufficient explanation. However, on *some* occasions the golfers were unable to stop their swing when the light went out just before the end of the backswing (about 0·40 secs. before impact). Reaction time in itself would probably not be a sufficient limitation in these instances. It is more likely that such cases involve what has been termed psychological refractoriness (Vince, 1948a). This phenomenon refers to the added delay in *addition* to a normal reaction time which must occur before a modification to a committed course of action can be initiated.   More explicitly, Welford (1967) in discussing the 'single-channel' hypothesis in man explains:

This holds that the central decision mechanism can deal with data from only one signal, or group of signals, at a time, so that data from a signal arriving during the reaction time to a previous signal have to wait until the decision mechanism becomes free.

Generally speaking, research work has centred around varying the interval between two successive signals for response $(S_1$ and $S_2)$ and noting the effect on the reaction time to either or both signals $(RT_1$ and $RT_2)$.   Under circumstances such as these, the types of delay encountered have been outlined, by Poulton (1966)* as follows:

. . . if the interval between the two stimuli $(S_1$ and $S_2)$ is less than about 0·2 secs. the response to the second signal (RT_2) will be delayed by about 0·1 secs. even when the man is half expecting to have to make a second response at this time. When the man is preparing to deal with the expected second stimulus as well as with the first, his response to the first stimulus (RT_1) may be delayed by about 0·04 secs.   It is as if the man reserved some of his computing capacity in readiness to receive the second stimulus, and so had inadequate capacity available to deal at a maximum rate with the first stimulus.   When the second signal (S_2) follows the first (S_1) by an interval as short as 0·05 secs., the man may on occasions be able to make a single response to the two steps.

The difficulties involved in measuring the reaction time under such situations are well appreciated in this area of the study of skill acquisition.   Not the least of these is the difficulty in differentiating the actual onset of a signal to effect a change in direction of an initial movement since this may overlap with, for example, inertial movement of the muscle prior to a change being brought about.   Other difficulties are imposed by the fact that some investigators have considered psychological refractoriness in instances where the successive responses were required of the *same anatomical unit* while others have been concerned with responses from *two different anatomical units* (Gottsdanker, 1967). It might be expected in typical ball game situations that much of the interest would centre around variations to responses in the same anatomical unit such as were attempted in the experi-

* Symbols in brackets have been added by the author.

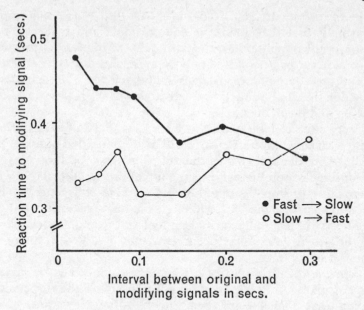

FIGURE 19

Refractoriness in going from:
  (*a*) a fast–slow movement
  (*b*) a slow–fast movement

Welford, 1967

ments carried out on the golf swing. In the main, evidence differentiating these two areas is not clear although work is ongoing. One recent study by Vince (unpublished) reported by Welford (1967) is of interest. Vince was able to show that a signal to slow down a response already begun fast showed the type of delays normally predicted while rather surprisingly, speeding up a response begun slowly showed no such delays (Figure 19). Although interpretations of these results are not altogether clear, Welford (1967) does suggest that:

> In order to slow a movement down subjects would have to change the patterns of innervation substantially bringing antagonists into play in order to arrest the motion. Speeding up, however, would have involved merely an intensification of the pattern already in operation.

Examples of psychological refractoriness are fairly easy to find within ball skill situations but have probably not been identified in this terminology by most players and coaches.

One of the advantages of confusing the display for opposition players is that they read the cues wrongly and make an inappropriate response. In the light of knowledge about psychological refractoriness, it will now be appreciated that when such inappropriate responses are made, it takes longer than a normal reaction time to initiate a corrected response. It pays to catch the opposition on the wrong foot!

Very often in table-tennis at a high standard of competition with attacking players, a player will have committed himself to a 'kill' before the ball crosses the net from the opposition player. If for some reason the ball hits the top of the net, the player will be unable to stop his ongoing action. He will generally be seen to complete the 'kill' although the final part of the movement may in fact indicate that he realises the inappropriateness of the stroke. A similar occurrence can be noted in many of the fast ball games.

Some of the ideas put forward can be summarised by saying that in ball games it pays to confuse or mask the display by doing what is unexpected from the opposition viewpoint. Not only will this make the input signals to the opposition less predictable and hence result in a longer reaction time, but the chances are that the opposition player will be committed to a wrong course of action. Under these circumstances, it will take longer than a normal reaction time to begin to correct this wrong action. The length of the increased delay due to psychological refractoriness will be determined by the length of time elapsing between initiating the wrong action and realising that it is in fact inappropriate.

Misleading the opposition in the sense being discussed here consists of altering the display in such a way that the opposition will make a response which in other situations would be appropriate (stimulus response compatability) but in the current situation is inappropriate. This is the basic result of introducing new strategy, positional play or team formations into a game. It takes time for the opposition to adjust their responses from what they normally expect to happen, to the new situation. Once all the teams are aware of the new idea, they can learn to read the new display and to cope appropriately. It is then time once again to change the approach. Thus, styles of play, techniques and strategies change from time to time and such changes are inevitable for a break-through in playing standard.

CHAPTER 4

Output Characteristics

So far, major emphasis has been on input characteristics and decision-making involved in perceptual-motor skills and particularly on the visual aspects of the ball in flight. In any fast ball game involving the hitting of a moving ball or even the catching of a ball in the hand(s) there is a certain dependency upon the ability to position the hand or the implemental extension of the arm accurately in space. It is not sufficient to know where the ball is. If it is 'in our court' we must be able to do something about it! This point was raised earlier in Chapter 1 when discussing the predictions involved in hitting a fast moving ball.

Legge (1965) has pointed out, that two factors are involved in such situations:

(i) the accuracy with which the position of the target and the initial position of the hand are localised.

(ii) the adequacy of the implicit response which must be prepared in order to move the hand.

Legge makes the further comment that:

In fact some skills including many ball games cannot be performed if vision is used to locate the effectors because vision is completely occupied with the target.

What constitutes the target for Legge is difficult to say. If he means the ball in flight, then his comments follow most of the writers already quoted and certainly there would be difficulty in watching both ball and effectors unless they were in close proximity—by which time, it would probably be too late to make any effective correction. If, however, the target implies the place to which the ball is to be directed, one would still find difficulty in locating the effectors visually as well as the target although it may be possible to direct vision from ball to effectors to target. A somewhat analogous procedure takes place in

E   55

billiards and snooker. Here the effectors, ball(s) and target
are aligned but, because of the spatial differentiation which
usually occurs between ball position on table and the pockets,
it is necessary for the eyes to switch from ball to target until an
effective position is reached. Serving in badminton constitutes an example of the eyes being fixed on both the 'ball' and
the effectors simultaneously. A similar set-up occurs in set-
shots from the field for basketball where ball, effectors and
basket are lined-up. Hence it would appear that Legge's
statement is too general and that it is only in some aspects of
ball games in which the effectors cannot be visually located.

The switching of attention from ball to target to effectors is a
relatively complex procedure involving the integration of
various sources of information. Thus, while this may be a
possibility for the skilled player, it would be expected in the
early stages of learning a ball game that players would need to
give more attention to acquiring the ball and to positioning the
effector than to the target. The beginner at tennis serving is
usually very happy if he manages to hit the ball. If it should
go into the right court, he is doubly happy!

As skill improves after periods of practice and players have
come to learn some of the constancies in the particular game
they are playing, there will be a transfer of some of the monitoring functions of vision to proprioception as Fitts (1964) and
Fleishman & Rich (1963) have demonstrated. The player
knows where the hand(s) or implement is without looking. He
can place it in position either on the basis of feedback information from the muscular system (kinaesthesis) or by a pre-
programmed action. A procedure of this nature is well
illustrated in the case of a player learning to catch a high ball.
Initially, it may be an advantage to hold out the arms so that
they can be sighted in relation to the ball in flight. As the
player becomes more experienced, such information becomes
redundant and the positioning action of the arms brought about
purely on the basis of proprioception.

The organisation of the implicit response is an extremely
important part of any highly skilled action. Such a procedure
can in fact be as much of a limitation, as a failure on the input
side of performance. Attention was again drawn to such a
possibility in Chapter 1. The learning of ball-game skills
involves the association of the right response with appropriate

situations usually on the basis of the monitoring of the display. It seems obvious that just as much difficulty will be initially found in organising the muscular system to bring about an appropriate response as in attending to the right input information. The marrying of the two involves an even higher level of organis- ation. In reviewing the literature on this aspect of perform- ance, Provins (1967) makes the following useful assessment:

> There is evidence to suggest that in infancy and for many years afterwards, a child spends a good deal of his time in learning to discriminate the muscles involved in bringing about a given type of movement and that the same thing happens in a novice learning a new motor skill (Bair, 1901; Landerwold, 1946). Such discrimination as Basmajian (1963) has recently shown, may involve discrete motor units, but once discriminated, the appropriate units still have to be selected for any given situation. It may be hypothesised that this selection procedure takes time depending upon the range of possible alternatives, in much the same way that the time for identification of a stimulus appears to depend on the size of the stimulus set or ensemble.

The last sentence reflects once again the 'information model' expounded in relation to choice reaction time in the previous chapter. It would certainly seem that in early learning of a new ball skill such an interpretation is a likely one. But, as was pointed out there, as stimulus-response compatability is brought about by a great deal of experience in different situations within a game, such a model may have limited application. Many of the actions involved in fast ball games involve ballistic move- ments. It must be assumed that these are organised completely on the basis of prior learning and once selected cannot be easily adjusted. In this respect, Woodworth (1958) draws attention to what he calls 'two-phase motor units'. Examples occur readily in ball games where the backswing forms the initial phase of the bi-phasic movement. It is generally accepted that such units are set-up in advance as a whole and cannot be influenced by current information monitoring. Such units usually involve short time intervals of the nature of 0·5 secs.

In summary then it would seem that initial relatively discrete movements become organised into larger programmes of res- ponse probably on the basis of the monitoring of feedback information from external and proprioceptive stimuli. Larger units of response often constitute ballistic actions which become preprogrammed as a whole and it is the timing of their application which is crucial in determining the efficacy of a response.

Replicability

In view of the comments made in the previous section, what is meant when it is stated for example that a movement (such as a ballistic movement) is preprogrammed as a whole? Does it mean that once the stimulus occurs for that particular response, it fires off in *exactly* the same way each time? Or, does it simply mean that the plan—what follows what in terms of sequencing of motor units—is the same but the timing of the firing of such units can differ giving rise to similar but not identical movement patterns? Little evidence is available from the field of ball skills. There is, however, useful evidence from other areas of athletic performance. Figure 20 (Adamson, 1968) shows two force-time traces obtained from an international oarsman at intervals of nine months. The very close similarity between the two traces is obvious even on a cursory inspection. They are not, however, identical as will be apparent if the one trace is superimposed upon the other. What does seem clear (and there are many traces of this kind to lend support to the argument) is that with an athlete who is highly skilled in a particular action (in this instance the vertical jump for maximum height) the effector pattern and timing of individual units from one occasion to another is very close. It is not unreasonable to assume that in this athlete's nervous system is a programme for this particular *complete* action. The minor variations from occasion to occasion are possibly due to random firing of neurons which form the background to any action. Or, they may be due to variations in the level of activation of the athlete from session to session.

It should be emphasised here that the action being performed is by a well practised (in relation to the vertical jump) performer. It does not necessarily follow that similar traces would be found in a beginner at this particular task. In fact, what little evidence is available, suggests the reverse. Furthermore, the vertical jump task is a relatively 'closed' skill in Knapp's (1964) terms. It is possible—although such a procedure would not appear to have been demonstrated—that a similar replicability of force-time traces would be observable

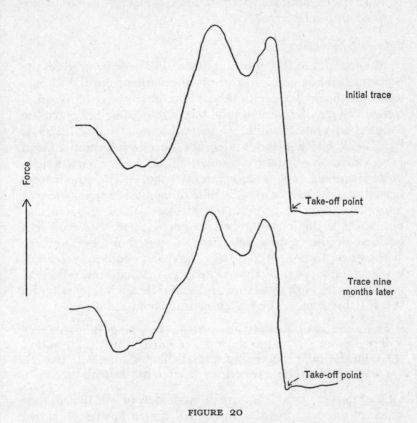

Time (76mms. represents 1 sec.)

Force

Initial trace

Take-off point

Trace nine months later

Take-off point

FIGURE 20

Force-time traces for a vertical jump movement performed on two different occasions (nine-month interval) by an international athlete. *Adamson, 1968*

in the experienced games player making for example a corner hit in hockey or a penalty kick in soccer. Would a similar finding occur in relation to skills which have to be performed in response to critical cues from the environment? Would a push-pass in soccer for example produce similar traces on different occasions or would the similarity be restricted to the order in which the muscle groups fire? The implication here is that variations in the execution of the skill are brought about by variations in body orientation of the player and in temporal sequencing of the individual muscular responses which go to make up the total skill-pattern rather than in a modification of the underlying 'plan' of the action. Further developments of this type of approach to the analysis of skilled actions are awaited with interest.

Efferent Information

Although up to this point, emphasis has been centred on the perceptual input side in terms of information from the display and from the proprioceptors there is another source of information which may be available and have something to contribute towards an understanding of the problem in hand. This is based on knowledge about efference (outflow information) and is an extension of earlier speculation and experimentation by both Helmholz (1925) and James (1950). The implication here is that the player may be able to monitor in some way the information which is given to the effectors and use this information to make his ongoing behaviour adaptive. The current position in this respect has been discussed by Festinger & Kirkpatrick Canon (1965) who have in addition produced evidence in support of the contention that outflow (efferent) information is both available and useful for spatial location by the visual system. Their argument is posed as follows:

> If in the central nervous system, outgoing motor nerve impulses are monitored and recorded, then information would also exist concerning spatial efferent impulses, that is a record of the specific directions given to the muscalature.

Of particular interest from the point of view of ball skills is that much of the experimental work in this area has been carried out on eye movements.

Monitoring of efferent outflow is not a new concept. Holst and Mittelstaedt (1950) made a similar proposition in relation to their work on visual motor coordination. They draw attention to the relative importance of actively produced movements of the body or parts of the body in affecting the pattern stimulation of sense organs (reafference) as against such changes due to variations in the external environment (exafference).

Much of the speculation and experimentation on efference in relation to spatial location has arisen from the doubts expressed by physiologists that signals from the extraocular muscles are used to any significant extent in the control of eye movements.

In a more recent review of human spatial orientation, Howard & Templeton (1966) have this to say:

> The eye has no joint receptors and, once the conjunctiva have been anaesthetised it makes an ideal organ for studying the role of muscle spindles and tendon organs . . . the conclusion is that there is no position sense for an eye on the basis of spindle and tendon receptor activity alone. But although these receptors cannot signal position unaided, it may be that they form an essential component in the direction sensitivity mechanism in partnership with the voluntary motor outflow. To test this hypothesis one would have to deafferent the eye muscles and test position sense with voluntary movements. Such an experiment has not been done.

Brindley & Merton (1960) have in fact demonstrated the absence of a position sense in the eye based solely on proprioception from the extraocular muscles. Festinger and Kirkpatrick Canon's work also demonstrated that in the absence of good proprioceptive information (characteristic of the eye muscles) the presence or absence of 'outflow' information makes a difference in accuracy of localising an object in space.

In addition to outflow information (about for example eye movements in tracking a ball) it is possible that this kind of information might be available for other aspects of ball skill performance. When for example tennis strokes are practised against a wall, the skill is much easier than that occurring in the game itself probably because the position, velocity and direction of the ball are more predictable. Why are they more predictable? Is it because the player can see where the ball is going and at what speed, or is it because efferent information is monitored and is therefore available indicating what effort was applied and in what direction? This does not negate the use of such practices, but it does suggest the need for a decision as to why they are being carried out. They may be useful for 'grooving in' a particular stroke pattern but even here, it must be appreciated that while such strokes may follow a basic 'plan' within the games situation, such actions have to be appropriate to incoming information about the ball, target and positions of other players. It is questionable whether a ball returning from a wall gives similar information to that which will be encountered within the game itself. The player may be learning inappropriate stimulus response patterns.

CHAPTER 5

Visual Factors

The fact that vision plays such a fundamental part in ball games has led many sports writers to talk about good players having 'an eye for the ball' or having a 'good eye'. If by this is meant that such players are capable of performing at a high standard in situations involving visual motor coordination where other players would have difficulty, there is little to argue about. But, if by this statement is meant that such players have particularly good visual acuity then the statements are at the least speculative. There is considerable evidence to show that many very good ball players have a visual acuity below 'normal'. At the same time, it must be admitted that there will be a level of acuity below which great difficulty will be experienced in performing ball skills and particularly fast ball skills. Some contradictory evidence is provided by Winograd (1942) investigating the relationships of timing and vision to baseball performance. He showed significant differences on the tests of directed timing, lateral imbalance and simultaneous vision between varsity baseball players and rejected candidates and non-athletes. Nevertheless, many of the university players in the study had poor vision.

It may well be that experienced players have 'an eye for the ball' in the sense that they are more capable of assessing position, velocity and acceleration characteristics of the ball in flight, taking in information quickly or making decisions on limited information. This may be due to an inherently more sensitive nervous system, to very fast reaction time or because they have been in the particular ball game situation so many times that they read the display more quickly and easily and respond in a more adaptive manner.

Graybiel, Jokl & Trapp (1955) reporting on the work of the Russian physiologist Krestovnikov relate two of his investigations concerned with the effect of exercise on visual acuity.

Tests carried out before and after a 1,000 metre race showed that while in the case of 27% of the athletes concerned visual acuity remained unchanged, in the other 73% visual acuity increased by as much as 45%. Greatest acuity of vision was found either immediately after the race or ten minutes later. It would be unwise to extrapolate from these findings to ball-game situations although the possibilities are of great interest. It would clearly be interesting to know when the phenomenon starts to make itself manifest after the onset of exercise. Perhaps physiological evidence can be established for the desire of many players before a game to 'get their eye in' by knocking up in a game-like situation! For although there are good players with poor visual acuity it is not unreasonable to suppose that increased visual acuity is likely to benefit any player.

Another difficulty from this study was the global nature of the concept of visual acuity. It would appear that visual acuity can be considered under four sub-categories which are not additive:

(i) Detection—the ability to state whether or not an object is present in the field.

(ii) Recognition—the ability to name the object present.

(iii) Resolution—the ability to discriminate parts of the object.

(iv) Localisation—the ability to judge the position of an object in space.

It is possible that if physical activity does have an effect on visual acuity it may be specific to one or more of the above factors. In addition particular forms of movement experience may have differential effects on different factors of visual acuity. An even more critical consideration in this respect, is the relationship between static visual acuity as normally measured in the laboratory (and presumably as was carried out in the Krestovnikov study) and what has been termed dynamic visual acuity by Burgh (1965). The latter has been defined as the ability to perceive an object when there is relative motion between the observer and the object. Burgh & Hulbert (1961) and Ludvigh & Miller (1953) have shown that dynamic visual acuity cannot adequately be predicted by performance on a test of static or standard visual acuity.

Another interesting finding from the Krestovnikov work was

on ocular muscle balance. The particular measurements taken were of heterophoria. This characteristic of vision is discussed by Weymouth (1965) as follows:

> Useful binocular vision requires a beautifully balanced or coordinated action of the opposing muscles to move the eyeballs in absolute unison. The visual axes must unite upon the object or point looked at. In looking about or in reading, the individual readjusts his eyes continually to bring point after point at the junction of the visual axes. When he looks at a distant object, the visual axes should be parallel. If this balance does not exist a condition designated as heterophoria is present.

The results of Krestovnikov's measurements on criterion groups of untrained students and tennis champions are given in Figure 21. Other tests showed trained subjects to be more orthophoric (tending towards zero heterophoria) than untrained ones. Of a group comprising 500 trained athletes (champion tennis, football, volleyball and basketball players) 68% were essentially orthophoric. In a similar untrained group only 40% were orthophoric.

Krestovnikov concludes that 'champion' athletes (in the widest sense to include ball players) have a more perfect eye moving apparatus than non-athletes. The conclusion that the

At 5 m. distance

	Orthophoria per cent	per cent heterophoria					
		0·1– 1·0	1·1– 1·0	3·1– 5·0	5·1– 0·0	8·1– 11	11·1– 14
194 untrained students	40	40·1	13·0	4·2	1·5	1·0	—
25 tennis champions	72	20·0	8·0	—	—	—	—

At 25 cms. distance

| 194 untrained students | 1·5 | 5·9 | 26·4 | 26·2 | 23·2 | 11·3 | 4·6 |
| 25 tennis champions | 8·0 | 56·0 | 20·0 | 8·0 | 8·0 | — | — |

FIGURE 21

Comparison of Phoria Measures. *Graybiel, Jokl & Trapp, 1955* presence of orthophoria indicates aptitude for the sports being considered seems to be more speculative. It is not clear whether the effect is a reciprocal one.

Greater changes were found in the same study on ocular musuclar balance after playing basketball and volleyball than non-ball sports. Apparently, these writers conclude:

> . . . the effect of exercise on the motor control mechanism of the eyes differs between sports that require repetitive action and play activities which are characterised by a continuous sequence of unpredictable situations which necessitate a more frequent oculo-motor adjustment.

Depth Perception

While precise judgement of distance of objects is important in everyday life, it is even more so in ball games—particularly

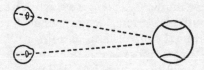

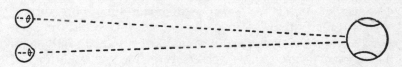

FIGURE 22

Convergence cues for depth perception for two distances of the ball away from the eyes

fast ball games where so many precise predictions have to be made. Depth perception is highly developed in man and is brought about to a large extent by the use of two eyes in stereoscopic vision. It would appear that distance is perceived in the brain on the basis of interpretation of convergence cues (Figure 22). Although such a procedure is useful in determining a *single* object such as a ball in flight or stationary, it does not function for more than one object at a time and at different distances from the eyes. For computations of this nature, the eye makes use of the 'disparity' which occurs between the images of the objects on the retinae of both eyes. Stereo vision of this kind occurs only for relatively near objects. With more distant objects (greater than about 20') disparity in the two images becomes so small that to all intents and purposes people are one-eyed (Gregory, 1966). There are other methods of determining depth which need not be considered here. Interested readers are referred to such excellent text as Gregory (1966) and Graham (1965)

What has been indicated is the importance of two-eyed vision in depth perception. This does not mean that with monocular vision depth cannot be perceived, but it does indicate the need for readjustment on the part of the individual and utilisation of other information from the display.

Again in the Krestovnikov study, thirty tennis players in one group were shown to have better depth perception than a group of 122 football players. Sportsmen were shown to be better than untrained controls and as a group the more skilful players perceived depth more accurately than the others.

An interesting finding in relation to depth perception and ball playing was put forward by Bannister & Blackburn (1931). They suggested that the wider apart the two eyes are, the greater will be the disparity on the retinae for stereoscopic vision. This may increase the ability to judge the relative distances of objects better or may mean that more distant objects (greater than 20') can be judged on the basis of such cues. While the average inter-pupillary distance (IDP) is in the region of 65 mms. these workers were able to show a range of 57–73 mms. in their criterion groups of 258 Cambridge undergraduates. Each of these men was assessed on his games playing ability (which involved a degree of subjectivity). Figure 23 shows the IPD in relation to games ability.

IPD	Games Ability		
mms.	*Poor*	*Good*	*Total*
Up to 64 mms.	78	44	122
65 and over	67	69	136
TOTAL	145	113	258

FIGURE 23

Relationship of Inter-pupillary distance to Games playing ability

Differences in IPD between good and poor players were shown to be significant. Further studies of this nature on more sophisticated players would clarify this issue. If such a disparity is in fact a significant one it argues for heredity factors in visual ability (Plates 13 and 14).

Eye Dominance

Closely associated with the concepts already discussed is that of so-called eye dominance. Experiments by Zagora (1959) suggested that by the age of three, the majority of children (about 75%) show eye dominance and that by the age of five about 95% become definitely right-eyed or left-eyed.

When talking about eye-dominance or limb-dominance the implication has been that the dominant member is on the opposite side to the dominant hemisphere of the brain. Since this is taken to be congenitally determined, one is normally talking about congenital left or right eyedness or handedness. However, it is fairly clear—particularly in the case of handedness that many congenitally left-handed persons become trained right handers so the position is somewhat confused. This has led to some workers (Clark, 1957) adopting the term 'preference' rather than 'dominance'.

Lund (1932) discussing the case of eye-hand adjustments calling for close coordination suggests that it would be an advantage in having the 'directing and controlling eye' on the same side as the 'controlling member'. In a target aiming test he was able to show superior performance when subjects used their dominant eye (the non-dominant being covered) than with the non-dominant eye. The best scores of all however were made with both eyes open suggesting that ocular dominance *per se* is not a simply explained phenomenon. Lund's findings were substantiated by Fink (1938) who found the use of the dominant hand and dominant eye resulted in the highest degree of coordination.

In more gross coordination tasks (such as would be apparent in the performance of ball skills) opinion would appear to be different. Adams (1965) in discussing the effect of eye dominance on baseball batting suggests that speculation amongst American coaches had led to a belief that the batter of the crossed-lateral type (i.e. left eyed—right handed or right eyed—left handed) has a distinct advantage over the unilateral batter (right eyed—right handed, or left eyed—left handed) because of the position of the batter's dominant eye in relation to the pitches of the ball.   Adams compared the batting performance of players from college baseball teams divided into two groups of crossed laterals and unilaterals.   The unilaterals scored better than the crossed laterals in most batting categories.   He also showed that the batting stances of the unilateral players significantly affected their performance in certain batting categories.   This led him to suggest that eye dominance may have some effect on certain aspects of baseball batting.

While these studies do indeed give support to better performance being obtained by unilaterals in tasks involving coordination, this does not mean that crossed-laterals cannot achieve a high level of achievement in ball skills.   Recent tests by Whiting & Hendry (1968) on English international table-tennis players revealed two crossed laterals in the top seven players and one who was indeterminate.

The question of dominance can be seen to be a confused one and it seems that many workers in this field have not fully appreciated the complexity of the problem.   Berner & Berner (1938) for example differentiate between what they term the 'controlling eye' and the 'sighting eye'.   The former is considered to be the one which guides the binocular pattern. Apparently the controlling eye is not always the same as the eye that sights in monocular tasks.   Using a large group of subjects, these workers were able to show that the controlling eye was the same as the sighting eye in only two thirds of the subjects (Benton, McCann & Larsen, 1965).

Schrecker (1968) makes a plea for the early development of 'approximate ambidextrality' defined as the ability to carry out the gross activities in which mainly large muscles of the arm are involved, with the inferior hand and arm as efficiently or at least almost as efficiently as with the dominant upper extremity. Schrecker point out that 'preference' or dominance of eye, limb, etc., is only a matter of degree and hence prefers to think of left-handedness not as the predominant use of the left hand, but as a consistent tendency to undertake new skills with the left hand rather than with the right.   An interesting study is quoted as being carried out by Grundlingh-Malan on 'The attainment of approximate ambidextrality in throwing'.   Two groups of 25 children around 8 years of age were matched for handedness.   Prior to the beginning of the experiment, Group 1 were accustomed to carry their books in the inferior hand and to do other simple routine activities with it.   Throwing practice was then carried out for a period of 6 months but whereas children in Group I were taught to use left and right hand equally in all the activities, Group II were allowed to give preference to their better hand.   Children were tested initially and after the training period for throwing distance, accuracy and other measures which are not of immediate concern.   The results of these findings are given in Figure 24.   The superior improvement by Group 1 in throwing distance was to be expected for the left-hand throw.   The gain in skill shown by the target-aiming scores was very much in favour of the group trained in approximate ambidextrality.

AVERAGE AGE	Distance Throwing Average Left	Right	Target Throwing Average (L and R)
JULY 1943			
Group I 8 years 2 m.	31 ft.	50 ft.	23/25
Group II 8 years 8 m.	34 ft.	60 ft.	13/25
JULY 1944			
Group I 9 years 2 m.	44 ft.	63 ft.	18/25
Group II 9 years 8 m.	40 ft.	68 ft.	14/25

FIGURE 24

Throwing distance and accuracy after a period of training in ambidextrality.   *Schrecker, 1968*

Peripheral Vision

Although the generality of Koestler's (1964) statement that:

The skilled soccer player keeps his eye on the ball, but is at the same time aware of the positions and peculiarities of the other players on the field.

might be questioned, it does draw attention to the possible use of peripheral vision in ball games.   It is a well documented fact that the periphery of the retina is particularly sensitive to movement.   If only the edge of the retina is stimulated, the movement and its direction are seen but the object cannot be identified (Gregory, 1966).   When a ball or a player is expected in the periphery of course identification as such may not pose a problem unless there are figure-ground complications.   At the extreme edge of the retina, stimulation may not produce perception, but it can initiate a reflex which causes the eye to rotate bringing the moving object into central vision.   Coupled with this is the slow reaction time to stimuli according as these deviate from the fovea (Poffenberger, 1912).

Experimental work on the relationship of peripheral vision to performance of ball skills seems to very limited.   At a subjective level, peripheral vision is nearly always deemed necessary for efficient performance hence Koestler's statement · above. Perhaps nowhere is this more true than in basketball where this aspect of vision is particularly emphasised.   A possible confirmation of the importance of peripheral vision in the sport of basketball is provided by anecdotal evidence (Weaver, 1965) on William Bradley (ranked world no. 1 in 1965):

> When dribbling, he wore spectacle frames covered with cardboard so that he couldn't see the floor (a good dribbler never looks at the ball)

and

> . . . suddenly rises in the air like a rocket seizes a high pass which seemed out of his range of vision, twist and lob a scoring shot into the dead centre of the basket.   Bradley can do it because he has abnormal peripheral sight.   As a small boy walking down the street and looking straight ahead he tried to improve his range of vision by picking out items in the shopwindows at his side.   Looking straight ahead now he can see 195° horizontally compared with a normal 180°, 75° downwards compared with a normal 70° and upward a phenomenal 70° compared with the normal 47°.

Interesting experimental evidence in sports other than those involving a ball have again been provided by Krestovnikov and throw some light on the problem.   He devised an elaborate test programme in which athletes performed various activities under conditions of normal vision, after the exclusion of peripheral vision, of central vision and finally when blindfolded.   Exclusion of peripheral vision for javelin throwers resulted in movements becoming clumsy and the distances thrown significantly shorter.   Performers also found it difficut to throw the javelin at right angles to the base line. In some cases blindness proved less of a handicap than did interference with peripheral vision!

An extension of this work to expert skiers showed minor difficulties of control after exclusion of central vision but with exclusion of peripheral vision a much more marked deterioration. Skiers experienced considerable difficulty in following the course and in judging distance.

CHAPTER 6

Acquiring Skill in Ball Games

It is necessary at this stage to remind the reader of the distinction made in the preface between 'education' and 'training' in relation to the acquisition of skill in ball games. The material presented so far has been directed towards an understanding of the components of skill which are considered to be of importance in devising any system of training in ball skills. The distinction is to be maintained in this chapter. That is to say, it is being assumed that the coach has a particular skilled performance in mind and will be setting out to achieve that end in the most efficient way possible.

It is reasonable to assume that any player who comes for skill training in a particular ball game, has some ball/bat experience to his credit. In this respect therefore whatever system of skill training is to be used, it is not being applied to naïve subjects. There will always exist in the potential ball-game player more or less highly developed general and specific abilities and skills. These may contribute favourably to the ball-game he is to learn or they may be a handicap. The player does not start performing in the new skill situation on a random basis, he already has existing response patterns, attitudes and preferences which affect his initial actions. In particular of course there are routines of maintaining posture, walking and manipulating.

The concern of this chapter is not with the laying down of foundations of ball/bat experience on which specific ball games may be built, but it is a topic worthy of comment in the present context. In the first place, it must be said that there is no firm evidence available which would allow it to be assumed that the establishment of a general 'pool' of ball/bat experience is a necessary or desirable prerequisite to the acquisition of skill in a particular ball game. Having said this, it must be equally well affirmed that learning is a hierarchical process and that future skill development is influenced by what has gone before. It would be difficult to produce objective evidence as to the most worthwhile early experience for potential ball-game players. It is not usually the object of educationalists to establish *specific* ball-game playing ability in very young children. It would seem reasonable to expect that experience of a wide range of ball/bat/player situations would be a desirable procedure if decisions have to be made. It should not, however, be assumed that it is not *possible* to teach particular ball games to very young children *if it is so desired*. The problem involves decision making and in this context is a philosophical one. Current sympathy would perhaps be towards the avoidance of early specialisation and hence in favour of ball/bat experience of a more general nature.

With these provisos in mind, how do people start off to acquire ball skill(s)? There are a number of different ways of approach amongst which the following three methods will be recognised:

1. Comparatively free experimentation with a variety of striking implements (bats, racquets, clubs, etc.), balls and players in an attempt to exploit their potentialities in a wide variety of situations. Under such circumstances, the person performing would generally set the criterion of success although particular objectives might be defined by the teacher/coach who might also give knowledge of results. This type of approach might well be used in the initial stages of ball skill experience previously discussed. In such a procedure, specificity of skilled action is usually less important than diversity of experience.

2. A development which proceeds from the specific to the general. Ball games are broken down into a series of skills, subskills and tactical situations. These are then practised in isolation or in small groups and the game is gradually built up from the isolated skill level to the composite game. As progress is made, more complex skill sequences involving groups of players may be taken out of the game situation and practised as a unit with the idea that when later fitted back into the game there will be a carry over from the practice situation.

3. An almost reverse procedure which progresses from the general to the specific. In this situation, the players are introduced to the game more or less immediately and specific

skills are acquired during the game itself. Any coaching
which takes place is always in the game situation and it is
considered unnecessary to abstract patterns of play for
practice in isolation.

Although these three approaches have been given separate
categories, it must be realised that more than one of these
methods may be included during the course of development of
ball game playing ability and also that particular methods may
be more appropriate to particular ball games. It is not
intended to develop the method under section 1 any further
since in the present context its application is considered to be
limited. The superiority of either method under sections 2 and
3 has yet to be established—both have their committed ad-
herents, and both have resulted in the production of highly
skilled games players. There have been few comparative
studies between the two approaches and it is difficult to see how
such investigations could be established with adequate controls.

If anything, there has been a discernible move towards
methods which span those outlined in sections 2 and 3 such that
skills considered to be too complex to be acquired during a game
are practised in isolation while the more simple skills are
acquired during play. It must still be recalled that when skills
are learned outside the game situation itself, there is still the
necessity for experiencing the perceptual cues which are
necessary for bringing the ballistic (or other) action in to play
at the *right* time. There is no reason to suppose, that this
aspect of the learning is any easier or quicker to be acquired
than the effector action itself and it may well be that acquisition
is delayed by practising the two in isolation.

Whichever of the above methods or combinations of methods
is adopted, a variety of approaches to training may still exist
within and between these methods.

'Imitation' in acquiring Ball Skill

No matter what general method of approach to the teaching
of ball game skill(s) is adopted, there will usually come a time
when it is necessary for the coach to demonstrate a particular
skilled action for his players to 'imitate'. This is not necessarily so, since there are methods of teaching in which the skills
are produced by the players in relatively unstructured situations.
The efficacy of such procedures in comparison with more formal

approaches has yet to be demonstrated but such an approach should not be negated. Even in such situations, some 'imitation' of other players will undoubtedly take place. In as far as the teacher gives an instruction as to the particular procedures to be adopted, he is attempting to conjure up in the mind of the player a mental image by verbal rather than by visual means. Much of what follows can therefore be equally well adapted to such situations.

The usual aim of demonstrating a skill is to produce some model of a required performance by some feature of the environment which may be deliberate or accidental (e.g. personal demonstration by a coach, use of film or film loops, watching others playing a game). Such a model is followed by a system of practice or prescribed training. In outline form, the following procedure would seem to be involved:

1. The player observes a demonstration of the skill by the coach or by some other method of presentation with a view to performing the skill himself at a later stage.

2. The player while watching the demonstration and shortly afterwards puts certain information (after suitable recoding) which he has abstracted about the display into short-term storage.

3. At that time and place or very shortly afterwards, the player is required to reproduce his interpretation of the demonstration. This involves decision processes and the selection of an already existing response pattern or combination of response patterns.

4. The player samples the internal and external feedback from his own attempts at the skill—often together with additional feedback information from the coach—and will usually make some form of discrimination on this basis between his own performance and that of the model.

5. The new feedback information received as a result of his performance is recoded and stored for future use or may be used in guiding his ongoing skilled performance.

6. On subsequent performance of the skill new decisions are made followed by revised executive commands in the light of previous feedback information.

The implications of such a procedure can now be examined in some detail. In connection with the first point, it is often said that the player 'imitates' the action pattern of the model. If by this is meant that the player copies *exactly* the movement of the model then this is clearly an error. There are a number of reasons why this should be so. In the first place, the model is often beyond the present ability of the player(s) performing. As Stout (1899) has stressed:

> Our power of imitating the activity of another is strictly proportional to pre-existing power of performing the same general kind of action independently.

This is one of the anomalies of the situation. A model is being presented which the subject is incapable of copying exactly and which he may never want to produce in exactly the same way! It would appear that in such a situation, the player is being made aware of possibilities for future attainment or of having a goal or sub-goal defined for him. Bearing this point in mind, consider now the player who is observing. The processes of selective attention and selective perception discussed in Chapter 1 apply equally well in this context. The player does not see all the display, but his attention and perception are selective on the basis of past experience and the current instructions of the coach. Once again, the importance is being stressed of the coach knowing what to emphasise—of what aspects of the display to indicate for selective attention and how these are to be perceived in relation to the performance of the whole skill. The orientation of the demonstration with respect to the players will clearly be an important consideration in this respect. It is unlikely that all the useful information can be got across by the coach or appreciated by the player(s) in a single demonstration. In a different context, Newell, Shaw, & Simon (1959) talk about 'plans' in describing the general strategy of a performance before the details have been worked out.* It would appear that a similar viewpoint would suit the present situation. The coach is trying to get across to the player a procedure—a rough outline of what follows what in the performance of the skill in question. He is not really intending that the player should reproduce the skill in the way that he has done it. He is trying to get him to reproduce a rough approximation to the skill in order that his behaviour may be 'shaped' towards the final required performance.

It would appear that models for so-called 'imitation' might

---

* Miller, Galanter & Pribram (1960) have enlarged the concept of Plans and the structure of behaviour in relation to skilled performance.

better be considered as being used for the purpose of 'social facilitation' (Thorpe, 1956). This term, developing from animal psychology would imply, not that the player is imitating in the sense of copying exactly but is being made aware that a particular movement is both feasible and desirable. What this really amounts to, is getting the player to discriminate an appropriate action as against all the other possible actions which he might have carried out in the situation.

The second point stressed in the outline procedure above is the recoding of whatever information the player abstracts from the display and the storing of this in short-term memory.* It is hoped that what is stored will at least be the 'plan' already referred to. In the present context, what does go into short-term memory store is some kind of representational information. (Although in the case of verbal instructions, the player may likewise store a verbal image. It is also conceivable that visual images might be elaborated by verbal support.) There is in the literature on the topic of short-term memory, wide acceptance of the idea of information being stored in the form or representational images (Posner, 1967). What is not clear, is the relationship of short-term memory to a more permanent memory store and whether like the latter, the cause of loss of information is the result of interference from other information (Sanders, 1967). When a player is observing a demonstration, it is most likely that some aspects of the display will be familiar to him so that an interaction between information put into short-term storage and information in more permanent memory store would be expected. It would seem that in a demonstration of a skill which a player is to reproduce in some form or other that the critical cues should be emphasised, that it should be repeated to give opportunity for rehearsal and that it should be practised as soon as possible after the demonstration to avoid spontaneous decay of the image. Where possible interference from other similar images should be prevented. This is of course difficult when a lot of people are practising a similar skill in a limited area.

* Short-term memory implies the limitations in capacity of the individual for immediate reproduction of situations to which he has been introduced (Postman, 1964). Typically, the procedure has been investigated in the laboratory by requiring subjects to recall after a short interval of time series of digits presented in random order and of varying length. At an everyday level, it is experienced in the difficulty involved in remembering a recently heard new telephone number particularly if it involves six or more digits.

The third stage encountered by the player in attempting to reproduce the demonstration he has observed involves a decision process. The subject has an image of a movement which he is to attempt to reproduce. A decision is made on the basis of how he perceived the model and a response pattern is initiated. When a player makes a response in such a situation, can it be said that he has learned that movement? This is a tricky problem! He could do that movement before the model was presented to him (at least in the sense that he had the physical ability to perform the action). It is true that the model may have suggested the need to combine several movement patterns in order to arrive at the correct one, but this does not alter the fact that the movements could have been performed before the demonstration! What has been altered and will be altered as skill develops is the relative attractiveness of a particular movement pattern which will be determined by the adequacy of knowledge of results (feedback) which follows on any movement, the amount of practice which has taken place and the player's capacity for improvement.

To summarise the position so far. The intention of a coach in demonstrating a skilled action or putting forward a model of skilled action in some other form is to get the player to produce an action as near as possible to the required performance so that he has something on which to work. The closer the initial attempts approximate to the required performance, the less 'shaping' that is required. Any methods which can be adopted to attain this end from demonstration to verbal mediation and 'guidance' so much the better. The advantages available to man in this respect can be appreciated more fully when one considers the difficulty Skinner (1938) had in teaching pigeons to play a form of table-tennis! The term 'shaping' has been used deliberately above as the process is at least analogous to the work carried out by Skinner (1961) on shaping behaviour in animals which precipitated much of the work on programmed learning. A start has to be made with the behaviour that the player is capable of exhibiting at the present time and by means of a suitable training programme behaviour is shaped towards the required model. It must be appreciated therefore that individuals will differ in this respect in terms of initial level of skill ability, in rate of skill development and in their final level of achievement, and there is no reason to suppose that a particular approach will be appropriate or the most beneficial to every individual.

Having had an attempt at performing the skill demonstrated, the player will sample the feedback. This will take the form of kinaesthetic feedback—the 'feel' of the movement—intrinsic to the movement itself together with extrinsic feedback such as visual information about the success or failure of the action to achieve the desired end. In addition, there may be augmented feedback supplied by the coach in the form of praise, correction or critique. On the basis of this information, the player is able to make a decision on whether to make the same response on subsequent occasions or to adopt a different movement pattern. Thus, as is well known, the development of skill becomes a succession of approximates in which the player attempts to discriminate between a feedback which is just right and one that is nearly so. The fineness of discrimination achieved in top level skilled performance argues for extensive practice. It must also be considered that hereditary characteristics could give rise to a nervous system which is inherently more sensitive in terms of its ability to discriminate so that in this sense at least, ball-players may be born and not made! As learning progresses, movements are organised into larger patterns of response often accompanied by a speeding up in the whole operation. The player requires to make fewer decisions. He 'knows' more clearly what he is doing. At a highly skilled level the player has all the time in the world to do what is necessary in the situation. In addition, the overall strategy is perfected, the stimulus sampling becomes less frequent, coding more efficient and different aspects of the skill become integrated or coordinated. Behaviour becomes shaped!

Discrimination

The term discrimination has been used frequently in the above description. As was suggested in Chapter 3, the development of skill is an ongoing process of discrimination. On the input side, it is a matter of discriminating amongst the conflicting stimuli for response and on the output side in discriminating 'the muscles involved in bringing about a given type of movement' (Provins, 1967). Following on these two processes is discrimination in feedback terms. The player must know whether his movement is appropriate to the situation and to what extent he may have to rely on reinforcement from others watching him play. Eventually, however, he must be able to discriminate on the output side. To 'know' when he initiates a movement that it is going to achieve the desired end. High levels of discrimination are perhaps more evident in the playing of musical instruments by experts. Critics talk about a 'flawless' performance indicating that no mistakes could be detected. It is worth noting, that in being able to detect a flaw, it is necessary to be able to discriminate between 'a performance which is just right and one that is nearly so' (Mowrer, 1960). It takes an expert to detect a mistake in the performance of an expert! (Not necessarily an expert player, but an expert observer—the two are not necessarily found together). This is equally true in ball skills as in any other skilled behaviour. When a fault is observed in another performing, the feedback may be equally emotional to the watcher. He realises how the player must have felt!

If a player is to discriminate, he must have something to discriminate against, i.e. there must be a model—internal or external to which he can refer his behaviour. If the wrong model is established, he may indeed be discriminating, *but against the wrong standard.*

'Guidance' in Skill Learning

The concept of 'guidance' in skill training generally implies either *physically guiding* the learner through the required movement pattern or *restricting* his possibilities for movement outside that required (Holding & Macrae, 1966). Implicit in both these procedures is that the trainer knows the correct movement pattern. This is not quite a complete analysis of the situation, because as Macrae & Holding (1965) have shown, giving additional guidance on a similar but not identical task as well as on the task itself may serve as an aid to discrimination by the performer and hence prove an efficient training procedure. These workers (Holding & Macrae, 1966) have also shown that 'hinting' (partial response forcing) produces satisfactory gains in performance. In this procedure, the performer is given an indication of the correct movement without actually being physically guided through the movement.

The use of guidance forms of training is a procedure often adopted by coaches although the above terminology may be unfamiliar. It is not uncommon for example for a coach to take the arm of a player learning tennis and to guide the arm through the required movement pattern (forced-response guidance). The extent of the backswing in a hockey stroke might be restricted by the placement of an arm or other obstacle in an appropriate position (restriction guidance). It will be noticed here that the two examples chosen have been limited to stroke production. While it is possible that these procedures serve a useful purpose in the acquisition of movement patterns outside the context of the game, there still remains the difficult task of learning the perceptual cues within the game itself which determine when the response patterns are to be initiated. Guidance does take place on the input side of skilled performance in as far as a coach makes the attention of a player selective. He is guiding the visual performance of the player.

A restriction procedure was used by Whiting (1967) in the experiment described in Chapter 2. In this instance verbal guidance was not used. The opportunity for viewing the ball in flight was restricted to particular areas of the trajectory. While this is something of an artificial situation as far as ball games outside the laboratory are concerned it does suggest the possibility that the use of restriction procedures of this nature might serve useful purposes within a ball game context.

Speed or Accuracy

The decision whether to emphasise speed or accuracy on the part of the player in learning a ball skill is a controversial one in the literature. Thus, Hovland (1962) suggests that if the criterion performance at both slow and high speeds is the same, initial emphasis should be on accuracy, but if the performance differs at high speeds compared with low, correct performance (i.e. that to be finally achieved) should be emphasised at the expense of accuracy. With respect to ball skills, it is not possible without an operational analysis to determine whether or not the final performance differs from the initial performance in any aspect and it seems likely that such a procedure would be different for different ball skills and depending upon whether the ball was already acquired or not.

Earlier work of Fulton (1942, 1945) on baseball batting suggested that stressing speed initially resulted in superior final performance. The problem is further complicated by

Solley's (1951) work on speed, accuracy or speed and accuracy in motor learning of a striking movement (ballistic). He suggested on the basis of this work that if accuracy as well as speed is important in the criterion task, both should be emphasised from the beginning. A more recent paper by Leonard & Newman (1965) indicated on a keyboard task that final performance requiring high accuracy was unaffected by instructions stressing speed during initial training. Subjects were apparently able to optimise their speed/accuracy performance to maintain the required criterion of speed and accuracy.

From these conflicting results, it seems likely that the speed/accuracy problem is task specific and decisions will need to be made either on the experience of the coach or by experimental work in the learning of particular ball games.

Mental Practice

The idea that mental practice* can make a contribution towards physical performance is perhaps a surprising one. It is, however, a common enough procedure and only another instance of psychophysical monism (the oneness of body and mind). Many players will have mentally rehearsed game situations and planned the moves that they would like to make in some future game. Such procedures might be put down to idle day-dreaming and certainly there is little evidence for the usefulness of such a procedure in terms of the ability to recognise similar situations in a later game and to adapt more easily, to make situations (particularly those involving fear) less surprising when they do occur or in motivating individual performance. There is an increasing accumulation of literature on the effect of mental practice on skilled performance and much of this involves the practise of ball skills. A book has even been written (Morrison, 1960) based on the principle of successful mental practice during the non-playing season in the game of golf!

Vandell, Davis & Clugston (1943) conducted three independent experiments to investigate the relative effects of mental practice, physical practice and 'no' practice on the acquisition of skill in dart throwing and in shooting basketball free-throws. Subjects for these experiments were matched groups of children

---

* The symbolic rehearsal of a physical activity in the absence of any gross muscular movements.

and college students. Amongst their findings were that daily directed mental practice of a motor skill of this nature probably improves the later performance of that skill. Mental practice appeared to be almost as effective as physical practice for the older children and students. With younger children, although mental practice resulted in better improvement than that of a control group, results were not as good as those obtained by direct physical practice.

Twining (1949) investigated the effects of physical practice and mental practice on the skill of throwing rings on to a peg. A control group performed 210 throws on the first day of the experiment and a similar number of throws on the 22nd day with no organised practice of any kind on the days in between (mental practice could not of course be entirely excluded). One experimental group performed similar test trials but in the interim period had practise trials throwing 70 rings each day. The mental practice group had similar test trials but their training consisted of fifteen minutes mental rehearsal of the skill each day. Percentage gains for the three groups were as follows:

Control group	4·3%	improvement
Physical practice group	137·3%	improvement
Mental practice group	36·2%	improvement

Twining concluded that under the conditions of the experiment both mental and physical practice were effective in producing significant gains in performance when compared with 'no' practice.

Clark (1960) using the Pacific coast one-hand foul shot as the criterion skill demonstrated similar significant effects of both mental and physical practice and was also able to show that intelligence exerted a statistically significant influence on these gains.

Other workers have produced essentially similar findings in a variety of different skills (Start, 1964; Steel, 1952; Ulich, 1967; Moody, 1967).

In view of the findings from the above studies it is perhaps surprising that more use has not been made of the technique of mental practice. At the same time it can be understood that vicarious participation of this nature is unlikely to commend itself to the activity minded player whose participation may be primarily dictated by the movement involved rather than the attainment of a high level of skill.

CHAPTER 7

Individual Differences

One of the most consistent findings from the experimental study of perceptual-motor skill performance is the widespread individual differences which exist between subjects, as indexed by their initial performance, rate of improvement or final attainment level. This does not mean that common trends are not apparent, but very often individual differences alone account for more of the variability in performance than any other factors which might be operating. Unfortunately, there has been little attempt on the part of experimental psychologists and other workers in the field of skill to deal adequately with these discrepancies. The position has recently been highlighted by Eysenck (1966) in suggesting that there should be closer cooperation between the laboratory experimental psychologist and the personality theorist.

Some support for the point being made here, can be obtained from the experiment by Whiting (1968) reported in Chapter 2. Both common trends in relation to some variables were reported but it was also necessary to draw attention to marked individual differences which occurred. In the chapter on Visual Factors, attention was once again drawn to the differences which existed both between and within different populations.

With this kind of evidence available, it is clearly necessary to pay attention to individual differences in factors which affect the acquisition of ball skill. It is not unreasonable to suppose for example that there are people who will never be able to attain proficiency in ball games—particularly fast ball games—although the number in this category is probably less than might be supposed. Certainly, an appreciation of this issue must make all teachers and coaches aware of the possibility of such differences and the need to take effective action in dealing with them. This does not necessarily mean that every prospective player must have individual attention, but it does

84

suggest that where large groups have to learn ball skills together, the environment should be so structured that optimal individual development is possible.

At a high level of skill development, it is quite likely that individual coaching will be necessary and this will be determined to some extent by the type of ball-game being considered. In some games, individual expertise is more important than social interaction and lends itself more easily to individual coaching. Where group-coaching procedures are being carried out, it should be asked not only what relationship the practice environment has to the game itself, but how are individual differences being catered for within the overall context of the group.

It might well be asked, what is really known about teaching stereotyped approaches to potential players? All too often the unorthodox player is successful in top level competition. From what has already been discussed in previous chapters, it must be realised that the unorthodox player already starts with a built-in advantage in as far as the display he creates is likely to be unfamiliar to opposition players unless they are aware of such idiosyncrasies. There are very good players who hold the wrong (?) hand at the lower end of the hockey stick, tennis players who play backhand shots with two hands or even change from right to left hand when dealing with forehand and backhand shots. Many top level table-tennis players play an entirely defensive game while others are predominantly attacking players. Height is an advantage in the playing of basketball but there have nevertheless been many internationals well below the height of 5′ 9″.

Examples like these could be continued *ad nauseam*, but by now the reader will have got the message!

Personality Assessment

The sphere of individual differences is usually subsumed under the heading of personality assessment or personality theory. This area of psychology has a long history and a considerable place in the literature. Some approaches are speculative while others are based on reasonably well established experimental evidence. Personality theory is concerned with the description of individual differences according to some structured framework. An attempt may also be made to explain how such differences are brought about and with the possibility of predicting behaviour on the basis of personality assessment. Many theoretical approaches utilise some form of classification—an attempt to group the multitudinous acts of behaviour on the basis of common underlying characteristics. Other theorists consider every act of human behaviour to be specific so that communalities of behaviour cannot be discovered.

There are probably as many definitions of personality as there are theorists so that any attempt to produce yet another completely new definition would only add to the confusion. It is, however, important to clarify the concept since the word is in common usage in everyone's vocabulary and there are likely to be differences in interpretation. Allport (1937) has defined personality as:

. . . what a man really is!

to this might be added:

Not what he appears to be!

By using this extended definition, it is possible to differentiate between what have been termed the biophysical and biosocial approaches to personality assessment discussed below.

The word personality would seem to have derived from the word 'persona'—the mask worn in Greek drama. Such masks enabled a person to appear to be something or someone other than himself. There is little doubt that people do tend to 'wear a mask' in their contact with the everyday world, and that if a person is assessed superficially on 'what he appears to be' misconceptions about his true self can be made. Nevertheless, a biosocial appraisal of this nature is useful particularly in everyday conversation. It is known on the basis of common linguistic understanding what information a person is trying to convey and in any case, it is the 'mask-like' behaviour which has to be contended with in everyday living.

Personality theorists may concern themselves with such aspects of behaviour, but in many cases—and particularly with regard to the theorists mentioned below—in as far as behaviour is mediated by nervous, muscular and glandular systems, they are more likely to think of behaviour in terms of such systems and to seek causal relationships in terms of interaction between such systems and the external environment. Such an organic or biophysical approach will be in the main the consideration of this chapter. In particular, the experimentally based work of Eysenck (1957), Cattell (1967) and Witkin *et al.* (1962) will be considered since it is the theories of such workers that have in the main been used in this context.

Both Eysenck and Cattell together with other theorists have incorporated the concept of personality 'traits' into their theoretical systems. This is a classification system devised to bring some form of order into the diverse acts of behaviour. Eysenck (1964) discusses traits as follows:

> Traits are not observable; they are inferred (as any kind of determining tendency is inferred). Without such an inference, the stability and consistency of personal behaviour could not possibly be explained. Any specific action is a product of innumerable determinants not only of traits but of momentary pressures and specialised influences. But it is the repeated occurrence of actions having the same significance (equivalence of response) that makes necessary the postulation of traits as states of being. Traits are not at all times active, but they are persistent even when latent and are distinguished by low thresholds of arousal.

Many traits have been isolated by different workers. These are often designated 'factors' of personality. Thus, for example, Cattell claims to have isolated sixteen first-order factors within the adult population which can account for most of the variability between people. If such isolated factors were independent of one another, the situation might stop there, but it has been found that certain of these factors tend to go to-gether—to correlate. On this basis, it is possible to arrive at second-order factors which reflect the correlation which exists between certain groups of first-order factors. Such second-order factors are often designated 'types' to emphasise the generality of their meaning. Thus, Cattell has arrived at two main second-order factors termed extraversion and anxiety. In a similar sort of way, Eysenck has arrived at extraversion and neuroticism. While there is considerable agreement over measures of extraversion derived from both theories, the concepts of neuroticism and anxiety are not equivalent.

It is largely a question of preference and utility whether a particular theorist concentrates on 'traits' or 'types'—on

G

first-order factors or on second-order factors. Eysenck puts major emphasis on types and Cattell on traits. This does not mean that Eysenck ignores traits or Cattell types.

The term 'type' can be misleading since it may give the impression that there are discrete types of people—for example 'the extravert' or 'the introvert'. Both Eysenck & Cattell talk about dimensions of personality or continuua in relation to both first- and second-order factors. A person may be classified as being at a particular point along an extraversion-introversion continuum or along a neurotic-stable continuum etc. In Eysenck's terms, extraversion/introversion and neuroticism are independent factors. That is to say that a person's score on the extraversion-introversion continuum cannot be predicted from his neuroticism score. It is then possible to plot the position of a person on a two-dimensional model as is done for tennis players in Figure 25 below.

With Cattell's system of sixteen personality factors—all of which form continuua—it is more usual to plot 'profiles' for people determined by their scores on each of the factors. Such profiles enable deviations from the 'normal' or other specified population to be quickly observed. It is also possible to compare profiles between individuals or between groups. Examples of profile plotting in relation to particular groups of games played are given below in Figures 26, 27, 28, 29.

While both Cattell and Eysenck* have produced physical measures for assessing their dimensions of personality, it is more usual to use pencil and paper inventories because of the ease of administration and simplicity. It should be borne in mind that such procedures can only give rough approximations to particular personality attributes and are usually restricted to experimental usage under controlled conditions. Their results should not be considered in any way conclusive and great care should be taken in making irrevocable decisions on the basis of such questionnaire information. With this limitation in mind, it is true to say that experimentally derived results under controlled conditions can throw useful light on population and individual characteristics. Such information may give rise to the development of new ideas or in the present context new approaches to training.

* Within the scope of this chapter, it is not possible to elaborate upon the theories and experimental work of the theorists quoted. Readers are referred to the major texts mentioned.

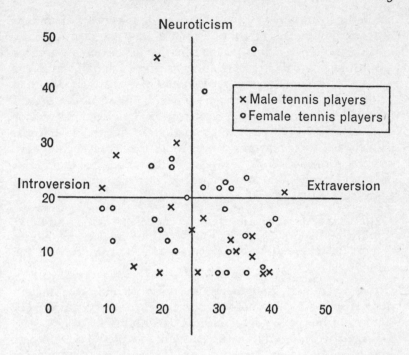

FIGURE 25

Personality scores of top-class tennis players. *Knapp, 1965*

Experimental Findings

Personality assessment of sporting populations is a fairly well documented field. Information is rather more limited on ball-game populations. It is not intended to give a comprehensive survey of all the available literature, but to select various studies which illustrate some of the points it is wished to make.

Knapp (1965) using the Maudsley Personality Inventory (Eysenck, 1959a), carried out a personality survey on a group of fifty-nine British lawn tennis players of national standard. The results are illustrated on the two-dimensional model in Figure 25. While the tennis players were shown as a group to be more extraverted and less neurotic than the 'normals' the differences were not statistically significant. Moreover—and this is an important consideration—although there was a preponderance of players with high extraversion scores, there were outstanding lawn tennis players who were towards the extreme introverted end of the continuum. This sort of finding appears again and again in the studies carried out to date.

Kane (1966) carried out personality assessments on three groups of football (soccer) players—professionals, amateur internationals and young professional players. He found a moderately acceptable profile similarity between the groups (Figure 26), suggesting a reasonably well defined profile for outstanding football players. Although from the figure it can be seen that these players deviate from the norm in being more surgent and controlled, less adventurous and less dominant, only the latter factor was statistically significant. Kane comments:

> Dominance is normally related positively with ability at individual sports but apparently, professional team players must be reasonably able to conform in the interests of the team.

A further finding from this study using second-order factors showed senior professionals to score high on the extraversion factor and low on anxiety (indicating stability).

Results from an American study on 270 West Point Cadets who were lettermen in American Football are reported by Werner (1958). These were compared with a non-athletic group using Cattell's 16 P.F.I. The football players were found to be more sociable, dominant, enthusiastic, adventurous, tough, conventional and group-dependent.

Cockerill (1968) used the Cattell 16 P.F.I. in a comparative study of low-handicap (0–4 inclusive) and medium-handicap (13–16 inclusive) golfers. The profiles for these two criterion groups are given in Figure 27. The only significant difference between the two groups was on factor E (submissiveness—dominance) where the low-handicap golfers were shown to be significantly more dominant. It is possible that the possession of a high level of this particular personality trait is responsible for the level reached by these golfers or it may well be that as golfers become more proficient, they also move towards a more dominant mode of behaviour. It is worth noting that while nineteen of the low handicap group scored above the mean on the factor of dominance, there were still five successful golfers who had comparatively low scores. While the possession of a dominant personality *may* be an asset in terms of high-level golf

16 P.F. TEST PROFILE

LOW SCORE DESCRIPTION	STANDARD TEN SCORE (STEN) →Average←	HIGH SCORE DESCRIPTION
	1 2 3 4 5 6 7 8 9 10	
RESERVED, DETACHED, CRITICAL, COOL (Sizothymia)	A	OUTGOING, WARMHEARTED, EASY-GOING, PARTICIPATING (Affectothymia, formerly cyclothymia)
LESS INTELLIGENT, CONCRETE-THINKING (Lower scholastic mental capacity)	B	MORE INTELLIGENT, ABSTRACT-THINKING, BRIGHT (Higher scholastic mental capacity)
AFFECTED BY FEELINGS, EMOTIONALLY LESS STABLE, EASILY UPSET (Lower ego strength)	C	EMOTIONALLY STABLE, FACES REALITY, CALM, MATURE (Higher ego strength)
HUMBLE, MILD, ACCOMMODATING, CONFORMING (Submissiveness)	E	ASSERTIVE, INDEPENDENT, AGGRESSIVE, STUBBORN (Dominance)
SOBER, PRUDENT, SERIOUS, TACITURN (Desurgency)	F	HAPPY-GO-LUCKY, IMPULSIVELY LIVELY, GAY, ENTHUSIASTIC (Surgency)
EXPEDIENT, EVADES RULES, FEELS FEW OBLIGATIONS (Weaker superego strength)	G	CONSCIENTIOUS, PERSEVERING, STAID, RULE-BOUND (Stronger superego strength)
SHY, RESTRAINED, DIFFIDENT, TIMID (Threctia)	H	VENTURESOME, SOCIALLY BOLD, UNINHIBITED, SPONTANEOUS (Parmia)
TOUGH-MINDED, SELF-RELIANT, REALISTIC, NO-NONSENSE (Harria)	I	TENDER-MINDED, DEPENDENT, OVER-PROTECTED, SENSITIVE (Premsia)
TRUSTING, ADAPTABLE, FREE OF JEALOUSY, EASY TO GET ON WITH (Alaxia)	L	SUSPICIOUS, SELF-OPINIONATED, HARD TO FOOL (Protension)
PRACTICAL, CAREFUL, CONVENTIONAL, REGULATED BY EXTERNAL REALITIES, PROPER (Praxernia)	M	IMAGINATIVE, WRAPPED UP IN INNER URGENCIES, CARELESS OF PRACTICAL MATTERS, BOHEMIAN (Autia)
FORTHRIGHT, NATURAL, ARTLESS, SENTIMENTAL (Artlessness)	N	SHREWD, CALCULATING, WORLDLY, PENETRATING (Shrewdness)
PLACID, SELF-ASSURED, CONFIDENT, SERENE (Untroubled adequacy)	O	APPREHENSIVE, WORRYING, DEPRESSIVE, TROUBLED (Guilt proneness)
CONSERVATIVE, RESPECTING ESTABLISHED IDEAS, TOLERANT OF TRADITIONAL DIFFICULTIES (Conservatism)	Q_1	EXPERIMENTING, CRITICAL, LIBERAL, ANALYTICAL, FREE-THINKING (Radicalism)
GROUP-DEPENDENT, A "JOINER" AND SOUND FOLLOWER (Group adherence)	Q_2	SELF-SUFFICIENT, PREFERS OWN DECISIONS, RESOURCEFUL (Self-sufficiency)
UNDISCIPLINED SELF-CONFLICT, FOLLOWS OWN URGES, CARELESS OF PROTOCOL (Low integration)	Q_3	CONTROLLED, SOCIALLY-PRECISE, FOLLOWING SELF-IMAGE (High self-concept control)
RELAXED, TRANQUIL, TORPID, UNFRUSTRATED (Low ergic tension)	Q_4	TENSE, FRUSTRATED, DRIVEN, OVERWROUGHT (High ergic tension)

——— Young Professionals – – – Amateur Internationals ——— Professionals

FIGURE 26
Personality profiles of soccer players. *Kane, 1966*

16 P.F. TEST PROFILE

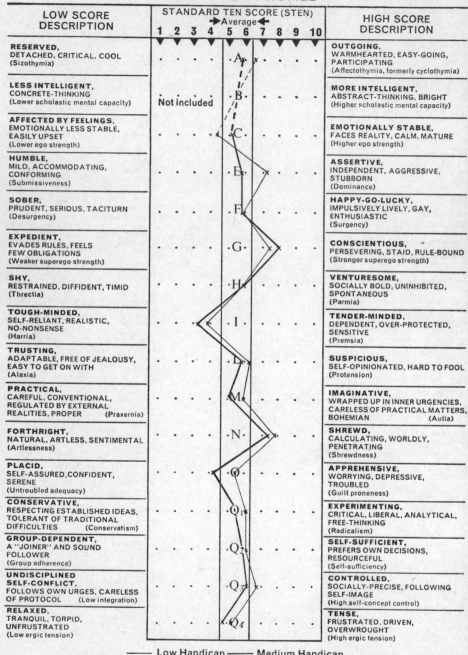

LOW SCORE DESCRIPTION	STANDARD TEN SCORE (STEN) →Average←	HIGH SCORE DESCRIPTION

FIGURE 27
Personality profiles of golfers. *Cockerill, 1968*

performance, it is clearly not a prerequisite. In the case of the medium-handicap golfers twelve scored above the mean on the dominance factor and twelve below. It would of course, have been instructive to have carried out a longitudinal study on this particular group to see to what extent the more dominant members had an advantage in proceeding towards better handicaps.

Sinclair (1968) compared sample groups of international rugby football players, county players and junior club players, again using the 16 P.F.I. An attempt was made to match the players for age (range 19–33 years), height, weight, explosive strength, social class and educational background but this was only partially achieved. The close similarity between the groups is evidenced by the data in Figure 28. Only in factors A and N were any significant differences found. On factor A junior club players were significantly different from the international players and the county players. On factor N the international rugby players were significantly different from both the county players and the junior club players. Once again, a complete spread of scores over the whole continuum for each factor was apparent for all groups indicating the way in which means scores can hide wide individual differences within groups. From the results Sinclair concludes that junior club rugby players are more cold, aloof, critical and suspicious (from factor A) and surprisingly, more sophisticated, polished, ambitious and expedient (from factor N).

Jones (1968) in a combination of subjective and objective appraisal of personality in champion tennis players allowed his subjects to list the five most important factors which they considered had contributed to their success. From amongst 47 factors listed, those of concentration and peak physical condition accorded the highest support. Technicalities like keeping the eye on the ball or position of the feet were judged to be of very little importance. Jones also attempted to propose an ideal profile on the same principle as the 16 P.F.I. for champion tennis players. This ideal profile was then compared with the profile of a great champion and also with the mean profile for 15 of the world's top twenty players. Although Jones reports considerable matching between the three profiles, this is not altogether apparent from the data presented. Other difficulties in this study relate to the population with which the individual

16 P.F. TEST PROFILE

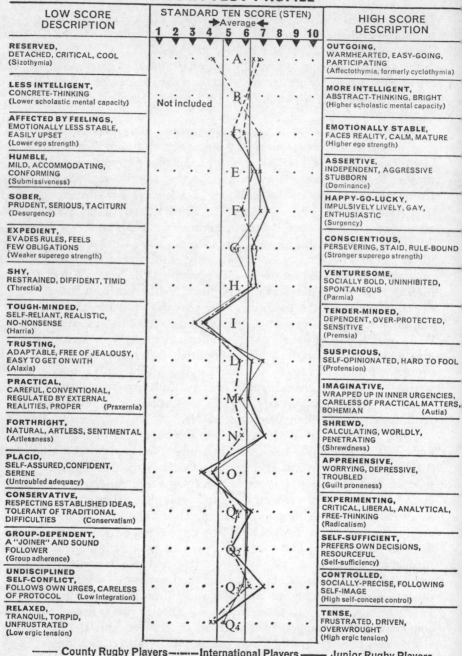

FIGURE 28

Personality profiles of rugby players. *Sinclair, 1968*

player and the ideal profile were related (Cattell's norms refer to American populations only). Again, the fifteen top players tested would presumably be of different nationalities so that their results reflect not only possible characteristics of top tennis players but reflect cultural differences which would normally be expected between populations.

Although the few studies quoted do show some common trends, the picture is by no means clear. It is obvious that care must be taken when examining descriptive information of this kind. That is to say, the idea of attaching a particular label or profile to a particular population. It is easy for a report to give an impression that all individuals in a population conform to a particular pattern if information is not given about the dispersion which is likely to arise on either side of the mean scores reported. Often writers draw attention to such factors, but it is more often left to the statistical sophistication of the reader. The point being made is well illustrated in a recent study on English international table-tennis players (Whiting & Hendry, 1968). In addition to other information obtained, personality assessments were carried out using the 16 P.F.I. Figure 29 gives the profile scores of the top seven players normed on the American General Population. The wide individual differences which occur even in this select group are apparent.

CATTELL FACTORS

SUB-JECT	A	B	C	E	F	G	H	I	L	M	N	O	Q_1	Q_2	Q_3	Q_4
1	6	4	4	5	10	3	6	6	8	4	5	5	6	4	5	7
2	8	5	4	2	7	3	4	5	9	7	5	2	4	6	4	7
3	3	6	5	10	7	4	6	1	5	8	7	4	7	8	6	5
4	7	6	5	6	4	3	4	4	10	6	10	9	8	6	2	8
5	5	8	1	9	9	4	6	6	9	4	4	9	3	7	3	8
6	6	6	6	3	4	6	6	6	6	5	3	4	8	6	5	4
7	7	6	5	1	4	5	1	5	5	6	3	6	7	6	8	6
MEAN	6·0	6·0	4·3	5·1	6·4	4	4·7	4·7	7·4	5·7	5·3	5·6	6·1	6·1	4·7	6·4

FIGURE 29

Personality profiles of international table-tennis players.
Whiting & Hendry, 1968

What is apparent from the studies reported and from many others of a similar nature, is, that if there are overall common trends in personality characteristics within selected groups of ball game players, it is still possible for players of widely differing personality make-up to achieve top success and it is perhaps a satisfying thought that this should be so. It is not, however, clear to what extent the possession of particular personality characteristics predisposes particular players to success in their game or what disadvantages have to be overcome by other players whose personality profiles are widely different from the population norm.

It would not be surprising to find that particular personality characteristics predisposed a person towards participation in ball games. The social characteristics of such an environment and the high achievement gains might prove attractive possibilities. Motivation to take part might vary with different personality profiles. Are there, however, particular personality characteristics which lend some advantage to such participants? Here the field is not very well defined, but possibilities can be suggested which may lead to future elaboration.

Often associated with the successful games player is a so-called athletic physique. Evidence of any conclusive nature for a relationship between physique and games playing ability has yet to be produced although subjective appraisal would give some support for the contention. The athletic body-type is usually related to a dominance of muscular tissue (mesomorphy in Sheldon's (1940) terms). A number of workers have attempted to show relationships between 'body-type' and personality characteristics (Eysenck 1959b). Although there would appear to be some relationship, it is a tenuous one and much less obvious than Sheldon's (1942) original work tended to suggest.

Personality and Perception

Interesting possibilities arise from the work of personality theorists who pay particular attention to perceptual characteristics of behaviour. In as far as perception is a function of learning, individual differences are to be expected. Theorists such as Eysenck (1957), Murphy (1957) and Witkin *et al.* (1954, 1962)—in particular—have placed considerable emphasis on this aspect of personality development. While a review of the literature in this field is beyond the scope of this book, there are particular experimental findings which are relevant.

Broadbent (1956) for example in relation to Eysenck's theoretical concepts has attempted to show that there are other interpretations of individual differences which might fit existing experimental evidence. It is not possible to develop his full hypothesis although it does read with interest. One tentative suggestion by Broadbent does merit attention. He suggests that:

> ... there is a minimum time during which information from one class of event is sampled before any action is taken about it. This minimum time is shorter in persons who are extraverted in Eysenck's operational definition of the word.

Possible implications here for such things as the amount of time the ball is watched—raised in connection with perceptual units in Chapter 2—will be apparent. Considerable individual differences were also found in relation to catching success when opportunity for viewing the ball in flight was restricted in the experiment by Whiting, Gill & Stephenson (1968). Further investigation of personality differences in this respect could be informative.

Eysenck (1947) and Himmelweit (1946) have indicated that the extravert is quick but liable to be more inaccurate in perceptual performance. However, a later study by Kiesler & King (1961) failed to find support for the postulate that extraverts are less cautious in their perceptual inference than introverts. More evidence is awaited before any firm predictions can be made in this area of individual differences.

Witkin et al. (1954, 1962) have been particularly concerned with the assessment of personality through perception. The concept of field dependent and field independent modes of perceiving is central to their approach. There is a suggestion and experimental evidence for the idea that people have a relatively dominant mode of perceiving. In those with a consistent tendency towards field dependence, perception is dominated by the overall organisation of the field while those more field independent distinguish parts of the field as distinct from the background more easily. Closely related to these dimensions is the concept of sophistication of body concept described by Witkin et al. (1962) as the systematic impression an individual has of his body, cognitive and affective conscious and unconscious formed in the process of growing up. Greater sophistication of body concept relates positively to greater field independence.

Recent studies utilising this theoretical position have

implications for individual differences in ball games skill performance. A study by Kreiger (1962) was designed to determine the relationship of figure-ground perception to spatial adjustment in tennis. Figure-ground perception was measured by the type of embedded-figures test utilised by Witkin et al. in their measurement of sophistication of body concept. (Subjects being tested are required to locate a simple geometrical figure within a complex figure. A time measure for a series of figures is used to obtain an overall score which relates significantly to the field dependent/field independent continuum.) The spatial adjustment test was devised by Kreiger as the measure of the ability of the player to move the racquet into position to contact the ball. Although a subjective measure was used for this purpose, it was made more objective by the use of three experienced judges. Results of this study indicated that figure-ground perception was significantly and positively related to spatial adjustment in tennis. The implication here being that the more field independent the player, the better his spatial adjustment in a tennis playing situation. Further findings were that field independence was related to spatial adjustment to a greater extent in more highly skilled tennis players and that men were significantly more field independent than women. The latter parallels results consistently reported by Witkin et al. While it is not clear to what extent field independence is a desirable quality in games players, it is of interest to find that there is a sex differentiation in this respect. It is conceivable that the male has an advantage in this direction. However, in as far as progress towards field independence is at least related to movement experience, it is possible that there is a reciprocal relationship between games playing experience and field independence.

Sugerman & Haronian (1964) have attempted to extend the study of the relationship between personality and physique in their examination of body-type and sophistication of body concept. Somatotype was estimated by Sheldon's revised method (unpublished). Sophistication of body-concept was shown to correlate moderately and positively with relative proportions of thorax and abdomen. It was suggested by these workers that participation in athletics in the general sense would probably lead to higher sophistication scores. Mesomorphy and body-concept score were shown to be closely related to athletic participation while ectomorphy was associated with a low athletic participation score. These findings can be related to those on body-type given previously.

It is still not clear to what extent participation in ball games contributes to sophistication of body concept or to what extent people with a greater sophistication of body concept play ball games or have an advantage in the playing of ball games. The issue is further confused because it has throughout been stressed that ball skills involving a ball in flight mean to some extent a dependence on environmental cues—one might say a field dependency. It is true that as skill develops some of the information monitoring is transferred from visual to kinaesthetic senses which might suggest a move towards greater field independence.

Abilities and Performance

Fleishman (1967) in an extended series of studies has related the concept of abilities to human sensory motor performance. In as far as 'abilities' reflect individual differences, these studies are of importance in this chapter. By ability, Fleishman means:

A more general trait of the individual which has been inferred from certain response consistencies (e.g. correlations) on certain kinds of tasks.

Because individuals who do well on one kind of task also do well on other tasks it is inferred that there are underlying abilities peculiar to all such tasks. Thus, the type of skills in which proficiency is attained and level of such proficiency will be determined by these basic underlying abilities. Some abilities may be assumed to enter into a greater variety of skills than others. Abilities to Fleishman are relatively enduring traits particularly stable once adulthood is reached. It seems likely that there are certain basic abilities which enter into a variety of ball game skills, but this has yet to be demonstrated.

Fleishman (1967) has also described ability as the capacity for utilising different kinds of information and in this respect suggests that:

. . . individuals who are especially good at using certain types of spatial information make rapid progress in the early stages of learning certain kinds of motor tasks (Fleishman

& Hempel, 1954, 1956) while individuals sensitive to proprioceptive cues do better in tasks requiring precise motor
control (Fleishman & Rich, 1963).

A possible link here with Witkin's field dependence/
independence and with Knapp's concept of 'open' and 'closed'

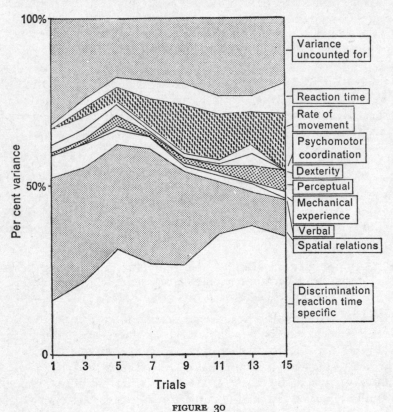

FIGURE 30

Percentage of variance represented by each factor at different stages of
practice on the discrimination reaction time task. *Fleishman and Hempel, 1955*

skills will be obvious.   In addition, the transference of monitoring functions from visual to kinaesthetic control which has been
stressed from time to time fits in well with Fleishman's idea that
abilities which contribute significantly to performance early in
the learning of a skill may not be the same abilities which
contribute to later stages of learning.   The concept is illustrated in Figure 30, which records the percentage of variance

contributed by different abilities at different stages of practice on a discrimination reaction time task (Fleishman & Hempel, 1955). It is results like these which have led Fleishman to conclude:

The repeated finding of an increase in specificity of the tasks learned indicates that performance in perceptual motor tasks becomes increasingly a function of habits and skills acquired in the task itself.

A reinforcement to the specificity principle previously elaborated and the need to practice a skill in context for maximum proficiency.

CHAPTER 8

Summary

One of the characteristics of the highly skilled performer at any task is the limited awareness of how the skilled action is carried out.   Such a person does not need to think about what he is doing.   In fact, if he does attempt to make his performance conscious he runs the risk of interfering with the smooth operation of the movement.   A further difficulty is encountered with ball-game skills in that many of the movements are ballistic in nature.   This implies that they are pre-programmed as a whole in the central mechanisms of the brain and cannot be influenced once initiated by information coming in from the environment.

One of the difficulties encountered by highly skilled players in teaching their skill to others is that they may not be aware of the way in which the skill has developed or the way in which it is carried out unless they have received some form of training designed to make such procedures explicit.   When asked 'how do you perform a particular action?', they are likely to reply, 'like this' and proceed with a demonstration of the skilled action at a level of performance which is above that appropriate for the particular situation.

One of the primary objectives of this book is to make potential ball-game coaches aware of those characteristics of skilled performance which play an important role in the acquisition of ball skill.   It would be wrong to assume that merely reading about these characteristics will necessarily improve the coaching ability of any person.   What it is hoped to achieve is a focussing of attention on what the writer considers to be the important characteristics in order to make potential coaches at least aware of possibilities. If success in coaching is to be achieved, it is necessary for coaches to recognise these characteristics in the practical situation, to study the ball game with which they are involved in the light of the information given and above all to make the necessary links between theory and practice.

While the primary concern here is with the acquisition of ball-game skills, much of what is said can be applied to the acquisition of skill in a much wider context. The systems analysis model on which much of the book is developed is sufficiently general to be applied within any skill area. It has been chosen partly for this reason, and partly because it lends itself to a structuring of those particular systems about which there is a body of experimental evidence.

Although all parts of the model are involved in the production of any skilled action, different skills can best be elaborated by attention to particular systems which are considered to throw the most light on the production of the skill. While early work in the skill area was concerned with the motor side of skilled actions, the current emphasis has been on the role of input information in the control of such actions. An important distinction is made in this respect between those skills which are primarily controlled by information coming in from the external environment and those in which almost complete reliance is put on monitoring of proprioceptive information for control. Since this book is concerned with ball skills which with certain qualifications are dependent upon the monitoring of external information—at least from the point of view of the timing of particular actions—considerable interest is centred around the input characteristics.

Consideration of the input side in the acquisition and performance of ball skills centres around the cues in the external environment which are attended to, the kind of information which is abstracted and the limitations which are imposed on the monitoring and processing of such information. The limitations imposed on data processing by the nervous system are considered in relation to findings from both the theoretical and laboratory practical situations from the field of experimental psychology. Much of the work in this area has centred around information theory—a development from the newly defined field of cybernetics. While this has been a useful approach—particularly in generating new research, its limitations in the present context are discussed.

It is regretted that most of the experimental results come from artificial laboratory experiments so that inferences which are

H

made do not necessarily transfer to actual game situations. This has been due to the very nature of the work involved and the difficulties of making observations in actual games playing situations. Nevertheless, the laboratory studies have been useful in drawing attention to those characteristics of skilled performance which are worthy of attention. There is still a need for making the transition from rigidly controlled laboratory experiments in which major sources of variance are controlled to field type experiments in actual game situations if useful inferences are to be established on any firm basis.

A considerable amount of the experimental literature in the skill area has centred around the concepts of reaction time and the related phenomenon of refractoriness. Such limitations on the processing of information are of considerable importance in ball skill performance and acquisition. While there is evidence for the fast reaction time of competent games players, this is only one of the limitations likely to be imposed. The decrease in reaction time with age points to the increased difficulty imposed in the acquisition of ball skills—particularly fast ball skills—at the young (childhood) age levels. While such a maturational effect on speed of reaction is fairly well documented, what is less clear, is whether or not a fast reaction time is the result of some hereditary characteristic in terms of a particularly efficient nervous system or environmental exposure to particular situations during development. In this respect, it has been found necessary to differentiate between simple reaction time and choice reaction time. While the former has been shown to be very little susceptible to training procedures, the latter has consistently been shown to change with practice. It should, however, be noted that much of the work on the training of simple reaction time has been carried out with older people when any training effects may already have been manifested. It is not clear at this stage to what extent early environmental experience contributes towards and affects the maturational rate of reaction time changes.

The whole concept of individual differences is given an important place throughout the book. The experimental literature consistently draws attention to the marked significance of such differences in determining experimental results. This does not of course prevent there being general trends within the results of particular experimental work. When one speaks of a born games player therefore much consideration should be given to the sense in which this might be conceived. If by this expression is implied that a capacity for playing games is passed on in the genes, evidence is to say the least rather limited! If, however, the implication is that some hereditary physical characteristics conducive to the playing of games have by virtue of interaction with early environmental conditions produced a type of physical ability/educability particularly related to ball games which make the person *appear* to have a natural aptitude at some later date, such an interpretation is more likely to find favour amongst modern students of heredity.

Some attention is given to the visual apparatus and its functioning because of its fundamental importance in the monitoring of information in ball games. Here there would appear to be greater possibility of an hereditary influence. But, at the same time environmental circumstances play a modifying role and it would be difficult to attach a label to the relative importance of either.

What does seem reasonably clear from work on personality characteristics related to ball skill success, is that while there may be personality characteristics which predispose a person to success in particular ball games, it is possible for people to achieve equal success with personality traits which do not measure up to some particular ball-player stereotype. It can only be assumed that such players are able to compensate in some way for the difficulties imposed by their particular personality characteristics.

In conclusion, the limited experimental evidence from ball-game situations which has been stressed throughout this book must be re-echoed. An attempt has been made wherever possible to draw attention both to general areas where research would shed useful light and guidance and more specific problems which need elucidation. It is hoped that this message will reach at least some people who are in a position to initiate such work and thus help to structure a skill area which occupies such a large percentage of the time of an increasing number of the community.

Acknowledgements

The following acknowledgements and thanks are due to:

Holt, Rinehart & Winston Inc., for permission to reprint a figure from Woodworth, R. S., & Schlosberg, H., *Experimental Psychology* (1954) (Fig. 17).

North Holland Publishing Co. and A. T. Welford for permission to reprint a figure from the *Acta Psychologica Journal* (Fig. 19).

G. T. Adamson of the Department of Physical Education, Leeds University, for access to original data and figures (Fig. 20).

The American Association for Health, Physical Education and Recreation for permission to reproduce data from *The Research Quarterly* (Fig. 21).

The British Psychological Society and J. M. Blackburn for permission to reproduce a diagram from the *British Journal of Psychology* (Fig. 22).

The Federation Internationale de Medecine Sportive and K. A. Schrecker for permission to reproduce data from the *Journal of Sports Medicine and Physical Fitness* (Fig. 24).

The British Psychological Society and B. Knapp for permission to reproduce a figure from the *Bulletin of the British Psychological Society* (Fig. 25).

J. Kane from St. Mary's College of Education, London, for permission to use data on personality of soccer players.

I. Cockerill for permission to use unpublished material on the personality of golf players (Fig. 27).

E. Sinclair for permission to use unpublished material on the personality of rugby football players (Fig. 28).

The American Psychological Association and E. A. Fleishman for permission to reproduce a figure from the *Journal of Experimental Psychology* (Fig. 30).

J. A. Adams and Academic Press Inc. for permission to quote from E. A. Bilodeau (Ed.), *Acquisition of Skill* (1966) (copyright: Academic Press).

H. J. Eysenck and Routledge & Kegan Paul Ltd. for permission to quote from *Crime and Personality* (1964).

E. A. Fleishman and Charles E. Merrill Publishing Co. for permission to quote from R. Gagne (Ed.), *Learning and Individual Differences* (1967).

C. B. Gibbs for permission to quote from an unpublished paper produced at the Applied Psychology Research Unit, Cambridge, 1954.

A. W. Hubbard and The American Association for Health, Physical Education and Recreation for permission to quote from *The Research Quarterly*.

Howard, I. P., & Templeton, W. B., and John Wiley & Sons., Ltd., for permission to quote from *Human Spatial Orientation* (1966).

H. Kay and the National Institute of Industrial Psychology for permission to quote from the journal *Occupational Pyschology*.

E. C. Poulton and the Editor for permission to quote from the journal, *Biology and Human Affairs*.

K. A. Provins and The Australian Physical Education Association for permission to quote from the report of their sixth annual conference, 1967.

The quotation from an article by E. W. Swanton was published by courtesy of the *Daily Telegraph*.

The quotation from an article by H. Weaver was published by courtesy of *The Observer* newspaper.

A. T. Welford and The North Holland Publishing Co., for permission to quote from an article in *Acta Psychologica*.

W. B. Saunders Co. for permission to quote from an article by the late F. W. Weymouth which appeared in Ruch, T. C., & Patton, H. D. (Eds.), *Physiology and Biophysics* (1965).

The *Observer* Newspaper (London), P. Dobereiner and photographer C. Smith for permission to reproduce photographs and captions (Plates II and III).

M. Braham of the Leeds University Department of Photography for the photographic work which resulted in Plates I, IV, V and VI.

A. J. Cochran of Liverpool University Appointments Board for writing the text which describes the work of the late David Noble (Department of Ergonomics and Cybernetics, Loughborough University) and which is reproduced almost verbatim in Chapter 3.

Mary Anne Louise and Angela Hendry for acting as subjects for photography.

I. K. Glaister of the Leeds University Department of Physical Education for helpful criticism of the manuscript.

Miss Robinson and Miss Wilkinson for acting as subjects for photography.

REFERENCES

(The figure in b ackets at the end of each reference indicates the page number in this book where the reference is used.)

Adams, G. L. (1965)   Effect of eye dominance on baseball batting. *Res. Quart.*, 36, 3–9.   [67]

Adams, J. A. (1966)   Mechanisms of motor responding.   In E. A. Bilodeau (Ed.) *Acquisition of skill*. New York: Academic Press. [21]

Allport, G. W. (1937)   *Personality: a psychological interpretation.* New York: Holt.   [86]

Argyle, M. & Kendon, A. (1967)   The experimental analysis of social performance.   In L. Berkowitz (Ed.)   *Advances in experimental social psychology*, Vol. 3.   New York: Academic Press. [1]

Bair, J. H. (1901)   The development of voluntary control. *Psych. Rev.*, 8, 474–510.   [57]

Bannister, H. & Blackburn, J. H. (1931)   An eye-factor affecting proficiency at ball games. *Brit. J. Psych.*, 21, 384–386.   [66]

Barbar, R. H. & Le Mar, S. (1930)   *How to play baseball.* New York: Appleton-Century Co. [13]

Basmajian, J. V. (1963)   Control and training of individual motor units.   *Science*, 141, 440–444.   [57]

Belisle, J. L. (1963)   Accuracy, reliability and refractoriness in a coincidence anticipation task. *Res. Quart.*, 34, 3.   [40]

Benton, C. D., McCann, J. W. & Larsen, M. (1965)   Dyslexia and dominance. *J. Pediat. Opthalm.*, 2, 3, 53–57.   [68]

Berner, G. E. & Berner, D. E. (1938)   Reading difficulties in children. *Arch. Opthalm.*, 20, 829–838.   [68]

Bolin, C. E. (1950) Batter-up. *Scholastic Coach*, 19, 7, 10–11.   [13]

Bradman, D. (1958)   *The art of cricket.* London: Hodder & Stoughton. [12]

Brindley, G. S. & Merton, P. A. (1960)   The absence of position sense in the human eye. *J. Physiol.*, 153, 127–130.   [61]

Broadbent, D. E. (1956)   *Perception and communication.* London: Pergamon. [29, 96]

Broadbent, D. E. (1965)   Application of information theory and decision theory to human perception and reaction.   In N. Wiener & J. P. Schade (Eds.)   *Progress in Brain Research*, Vol. 17. Amsterdam: Elsevier Pub. Co.   [46]

Brown, J. F. (1931)   The visual perception of velocity. *Psych. Forsch.*, 14, 199.   [16]

Burgh, A. (1965)   Apparatus for measurement of dynamic visual acuity. *Percep. & Mot. Skills*, 20, 231–234.   [63]

Burgh, A. & Hulbert, S. F. (1961)   Dynamic visual acuity as related to age, sex and static acuity. *J. Appl. Psych.*, 45, 111–116.   [63]

Cattell, R. B. (1967)   *The scientific analysis of personality.* London: Pelican Books.   [87]

Chapman, L. E. & Severeid, H. (1941)   *Play ball.* New York: Harper Bros.   [13]

Chernikoff, R. & Taylor, F. V. (1952) Reaction time to kin-aesthetic stimulation resulting from sudden arm displacement. *J. Exp. Psych.*, 43, 1–8. [37]

Clark, L. V. (1960) Effect of mental practice on the development of a certain motor skill. *Res. Quart.*, 31, 560–569. [83]

Clark, M. M. (1957) *Left handedness.* London: U.L.P. [67]

Cockerill, I. (1968) Personality of golf players. Advanced Diploma in Physical Education Thesis, University of Leeds. [90]

Craik, K. J. W. (1947) Theory of the human operator in control systems I. *Brit. J. Psych.*, 28, 56–61. [17]

Crossman, E. R. F. W. (1955) The measurement of discimin-ability. *Q. J. Exp. Psych.*, 7, 176–195. [46]

Denenberg, V. H. (1953) A simplified method of measuring kin-aesthetic reaction time. *Am. J. Psych.*, 66, 309–311. [37]

Dobereiner, P. (1967) Why the camera is a blinking liar. London: *Observer*, Dec. 17th, 1967. [12]

Eastwood, P., Entwhistle, P., Gill, B. & Stephenson, J. (1968) Relation of reaction time and movement time within a physical education context. Advanced Diploma in Physical Education Thesis, University of Leeds. [43]

Eysenck, H. J. (1947) *Dimensions of personality.* London: Rout-ledge & Kegan Paul. [9]

Eysenck, H. J. (1957) *Dynamics of Anxiety and hysteria.* London: Routledge & Kegan Paul. [87, 96]

Eysenck, H. J. (1959a) *Manual of the Maudsley Personality Inventory.* London: U.L.P. [89]

Eysenck, H. J. (1959b) The Rees-Eysenck body index and Shel-don's somatotype system. *J. Ment. Sc.*, 105, 1053–1058. [96]

Eysenck, II. J. (1964) *Crime and Personality.* London: Routledge & Kegan Paul. [87]

Eysenck, H. J. (1966) Personality and Experimental psychology. *Bull. Brit. Psych. Soc.*, 19, 62, 1–28. [84]

Festinger, L. & Kirkpatrick Canon, L. (1965) Information about spatial location based on knowledge about efference. *Psych. Rev.*, 72, 373–384. [60]

Fink, W. H. (1938) The dominant eye: its clinical significance. *Arch. Opthalm.*, 19, 555–582. [67]

Fitts, P. M., Bahrick, H. P., Noble, M. E., & Briggs, A. E. (1961) *Skilled Performance.* New York: Wiley & Co. [17]

Fitts, P. M. (1964) Perceptual-motor skill learning. In A. W. Melton (Ed.) *Categories of Human Learning.* London: Academic Press. [2, 11, 56]

Fleishman, E. A. & Hempel, W. E. (1954) Changes in factor structure of a complex psychomotor test as a function of practice. *Psychometrika*, 18, 239–252. [100]

Fleishman, E. A. & Hempel, W. E. (1955) The relation between abilities and improvement with practice in a visual discrimi-nation reaction task. *J. Exp. Psych.*, 49, 301–312. [100, 101]

Fleishman, E. A. & Hempel, W. E. (1956) Factorial analysis of complex psychomotor performance and related skills. *J. Appl. Psych.*, 40, 96–104. [100]

Fleishman, E. A. & Rich, S. (1963) Role of kinaesthetic and spatial visual abilities in perceptual motor learning. *J. Exp. Psych.*, 66, 6–11. [14, 56, 100]

Fleishman, E. A. (1967) Individual differences and motor learning. In Gagne, R. M. (Ed.) *Learning and individual differences.* Ohio: Merrill. [99]

Ford, A., White, C. T., & Lichtenstein, M. (1959) Analysis of eye movements during free search. *J. Opt. Soc. Am.*, 49, 287–292. [20]

Fraser, N. (1962) *Power tennis.* London: Stanley Paul. [13]

Fuchs, A. H. (1962) The progression-regression hypothesis in perceptual-motor skill learning. *J. Exp. Psych.*, 623, 177–182. [17]

Fulton, R. (1942) Speed and accuracy in learning a ballistic movement. *Res. Quart.*, 13, 30–36. [81]

Fulton, R. (1945) Speed and accuracy in learning movements. *Arch. Psych.*, 41. [81]

Garvey, W. D. & Mitnick, L. L. (1957) An analysis of tracking behaviour in terms of lead-lag errors. *J. Exp. Psych.*, 53, 373–378. [17]

Gibbs, C. B. (1954) Servo principles in sensory organisation and the transfer of skill. Applied Psychology Research Unit Publication, Cambridge. [16]

Gibson, M. A., Karpovich, P. V. & Gollnick, P. D. (1961) Effect of training upon reflex and reaction time. Unpublished paper, Dept. of Physiology, Springfield College, Massachusetts. [38]

Goodenough, F. L. (1935) The development of the reactive processes from childhood to maturity. *J. Exp. Psych.*, 18, 431–450. [43]

Gottsdanker, R. (1967) Computer determination of the effect of superseding signals. *Acta. Psych.*, Vol. 27, 35–44. [52]

Graham, C. H. (Ed.) (1965) *Vision and visual perception.* New York: Wiley. [66]

Gregory, R. L. (1966) *Eye and brain.* London: Weidenfield & Nicolson. [6, 66, 70]

Graybiel, A., Jokl, E. & Trapp, C. (1955) Russian studies of vision in relation to physical activity and sports. *Res. Quart.*, 36, 480–485. [62]

Hankinson, J. T. (1951) *Hockey for schools.* London: Allen & Unwin. [13]

Helmholz, H. (1925) *Treatise on physiological optics* (3rd ed.), Vol. 3. Wisconsin: Optical Society of America. [60]

Hick, W. E. & Bates, J. A. V. (1948) *The human operator of control mechanisms.* Ministry of Supply permanent records of research and development, No. 17. [41]

Hick, W. E. (1952) On the rate of gain of information. *Q. J. Exp. Psych.*, 4, 11–26. [46]

Himmelweit, H. T. (1946) Speed and accuracy of work as related to temperament. *Brit. J. Psych.*, 36, 132–144. [97]

Holding, D. H. & Macrae, A. W. (1964) Guidance, restriction

and knowledge of results. *Ergonomics*, 7, 3, 289–295. [80]

Holding, D. H. (1962) Transfer between difficult and easy tasks. *Brit. J. Psych.*, 53, 4, 397–407. [ix]

Holding, D. H. (1966) *Principles of Training*. London: Pergamon. [7]

Holding, D. H. & Macrae, A. W. (1966) Rate and force of guidance in perceptual-motor tasks with reversed or random spatial correspondence. *Ergonomics*, 9, 4, 289–296. [80]

Holst, E. Von & Mittelstaedt, H. (1950) Das reafferenzprinzip. *Naturwissenschaften.*, 37, 464–476. [60]

Horn, G. (1966) Physiological and psychological aspects of selective perception. In D. S. Lehrman, R. A. Hinde, & E. Shaw (Eds.) *Advances in the study of behaviour*, Vol. 1. New York: Academic Press. [6]

Hovland, C. I. (1963) Human learning and retention. In S. S. Stevens (Ed.) *Handbook of experimental psychology*. New York: Wiley. [81]

Howard, I. P. & Templeton, W. B. (1966) *Human spatial orientation*. London: Wiley. [6]

Hubbard, A. W. & Seng, C. N. (1954) Visual movements of batters. *Res. Quart.*, 25, 42–57. [13, 21, 34, 38]

James, W. (1950) *Principles of psychology*, Vol. 2. New York: Dover. [60]

Jessee, D. E. (1939) *Baseball*. New York: Barnes & Co. [13]

Jones, H. E. (1937) Reaction time and motor development. *Am. J. Psych.*, 50, 181–194. [43]

Jones, C. M. (1968) *Tennis: how to become a champion*. London: Faber. [93]

Kane, J. (1966) Personality description of soccer ability. *Res. Phys. Ed.*, 1, 2, 54–64. [90]

Kay, H. (1957) Information theory in the understanding of skills. *Occ. Psych.*, 31, 1, 218–224. [17]

Kiesler, C. A. & King, G. F. (1961) Individual differences in making perceptual inferences. *Percep. & Mort. Skills*, 13, 3–6. [97]

Knapp, B. et al. (1961) Simple reaction time of selected top-class sportsman and research students. *Res. Quart.*, 32, 3, 409–412. [41]

Knapp, B. (1964) *Skill in sport*. London: Routledge & Kegan Paul. [1, 9]

Knapp, B. (1965) The personality of lawn tennis players. *Bull. Brit. Psych. Soc.*, 18, 61, 1–3. [89]

Koestler, A. (1964) *The act of creation*. London: Hutchinson. [69]

Kreiger, J. C. (1962) The influence of figure-ground perception on spatial adjustment in tennis. M.Sc. thesis Univ. of Calif. at Los Angeles. [98]

Laming, D. R. J. (1962) A statistical test of a prediction from information theory in a card-sorting situation. *Q.J. Exp. Psych.*, 14, 34–48. [46]

Landerwold, A. J. S. (1945) Electromyographic investigations of position and manner of working in typewriting. *Acta. Physiol. Scand.*, 24, Supp. 84. [57]

Lange, L. (1888)   Neue experimente uber den Vorgang derein-fachen reaction auf Sinnesreizen.   *Philos. Stud.*, 4, 479–510. [41]

Legge, D. (1965)   Analysis of visual and proprioceptive components of motor skill by means of a drug. *Brit. J. Psych.*, 56, 243–256. [55]

Leonard, J. (1959)   Tactual Choice Reactions: I.   *Q. J. Exp. Psych.*, 11, 76–83.   [46]

Leonard, J. A. & Newman, R. C. (1965)   On the acquisition and maintenance of high speed and high accuracy in a keyboard task.   *Ergonomics*, 8, 3, 281–304.   [82]

Ludvigh, E. & Miller, J. W. (1953)   A study of dynamic visual acuity.   USN Sch. Aviat. Med. joint project. Rep., No. NM 001 075.01.01.   [63]

Lund, F. H. (1932)   The dependence of eye-hand coordinations upon eye dominance.   *Am. J. Psych.*, 44, 756–762.   [67]

Mackworth, J. F. & Mackworth, N. H. (1958)   Eye fixation recorded on changing visual scenes by the television eye-marker. *J. Opt. Soc. Am.*, 48, 7, 439–443.   [20]

McCool, C. (1961)   The best way to play cricket.   London: *Daily Mirror.*   [13]

Macrae, A. W. & Holding, D. H. (1965)   Method and task in motor guidance.   *Ergonomics*, 8, 315–320.   [80]

Meissner, E. E. & Meyers, E. Y. (1950)   *Basketball for girls.*   New York: Barnes.   [13]

Meredith, G. P. (1966)   *Instruments of communication.*   London: Pergamon.   [ix]

Miller, G. A., Galanter, E., & Pribram, K. H. (1960)   *Plans and the structure of behaviour.*   New York: Holt, Rinehart & Winston.   [76]

Miller, R. G. & Shay, C. T. (1964)   Relativity of reaction time to the speed of a softball.   *Res. Quart.*, 35, 433–437.   [41, 42]

Milhorn, H. T. (1966)   *The application of control theory to physiological systems.*   London: Saunders.   [7]

Moody, D. L. (1967)   Imagery differences in women of varying levels of experience.   *Res. Quart.*, 38, 3.   [83]

Morgan, C. T. & King, R. A. (1966)   *Introduction to psychology.* New York: McGraw Hill.   [3]

Morgan, J. (1953)   *Squash racquets for women.*   London: Sporting Handbooks.   [13, 15]

Morrison, A. J. (1960)   *Golf without practice.*   New York: Simon & Schuster.   [82]

Moss, E. (1956)   *Lawn tennis: how to discover and correct faults.* London: Link House Publications.   [13, 14, 15]

Mottram, A. (1966) *Improve your tennis.* London: Penguin Books. [13]

Mowrer, O. H. (1941)   Preparatory set (expectancy)—further evidence of its central locus.   *J. Exp. Psych.*, 28, 116–133.   [41]

Mowrer, O. H. (1960)   *Learning theory and behaviour.*   New York: Wiley.   [41, 80]

Murphy, G. (1957)   *Personality: a biosocial approach to origins and structure.*   New York: Harper.   [96]

Newell, A., Shaw, J. C., & Simon, H. A. (1959)   A report on a general problem solving program. *Proceedings of the international conference on Information Processing,* Paris. [76]

Noble, C. E. (1966) Selective learning. In E. A. Bilodeau (Ed.) *Acquisition of skill.* New York: Academic Press. [15]

Noble, D. (1966) Unpublished data. Loughborough University of Technology. [49]

Osgood, C. E. (1964) *Method and theory in experimental psychology.* New York: Oxford University Press. [ix, 14]

Pawle, G. (1951) *Squash racquets.* London: Ward, Lock & Co. [13]

Poffenberger, A. T. (1912) Reaction time to retinal stimulation with special reference to the time lost in conduction through nerve centres. *Arch. Psych.,* New York, 23. [70]

Posner, M. I. (1967) Short-term memory systems in human information processing. *Acta. Psych.,* 27, 267–284. [77]

Postman, L. (1964) Short-term memory and incidental learning. In A. W. Melton (Ed.) *Categories of Human learning.* New York: Academic Press. [77]

Poulton, E. C. (1957) On prediction in skilled movements. *Psych. Bull.,* 54, 6, 467–478. [9]

Poulton, E. C. (1965) Skill in fast ball games. *Biology and Human Affairs,* 31, 1, 1–5. [11, 38, 41]

Poulton, E. C. (1966) Tracking behaviour. In E. A. Bilodeau (Ed.) *Acquisition of Skill.* London: Academic Press.

Provins, K. (1967) Some recent advances in the study of motor skills. Report of the sixth national conference in physical education. Adelaide: Australian P. E. Assoc. [57, 79]

Rabbitt, P. M. (1967) Learning to ignore irrelevant information. *Am. J. Psych.,* 80, 1, 1–13. [6]

Rangecroft, C. (1961) *The right way to play badminton.* Surrey: Elliotts. [12]

Ruch, T. C. (1951) Motor Systems. In S. S. Stevens (Ed.) *Handbook of Experimental Psychology.* New York: Wiley. [15]

Sanders, A. F. (1967) Short-term memory and information processing. *Acta. Psych.,* 27, 265–266. [77]

Schrecker, K. A. (1968) Approximate ambidexterity—why and how? *J. of Sports Medicine & Physical Fitness,* 8, 1, 44–48. [68]

Scott, M. G. (1945) *Analysis of human motion.* New York: Crofts. [42]

Shackel, B. (1960) Electro-oculography. Proceedings of the third international conference on medical electronics. London: 1960. [20]

Shackel, B. & Whitfield, D. (1963) Instruments and people. *Ergonomics for industry: 2.* Pamphlet published by the D.S.I.R. information division. [4]

Shallice, T. (1964) The detection of change and the perceptual-moment hypothesis. *Brit. J. Stats. Psych.,* XVII, 113–135. [30]

Sheldon, W. H., Stevens, S. S., & Tucker, W. B. (1940) *The varieties of human physique.* New York: Harper. [96]

Sheldon, W. H. & Stevens, S. S. (1942) *The varieties of temperament.* New York: Harper. [96]

Sinclair, E. (1968) Personality of rugby football players. Advanced Diploma in Physical Education, Thesis, University of Leeds. [93]

Singleton, W. T. (1967) Ergonomics in systems design. *Ergonomics*, 10, 5, 541–548. [2]

Skinner, B. F. (1938) *The behaviour of organisms*. New York: Appleton-Century Crofts. [78]

Skinner, B. F. (1961) *Cumulative Record*. New York: Appleby. [78]

Slater-Hammel, A. T. & Stumpner, R. L. (1950) Batting reaction time. *Res. Quart.*, 21, 353–356. [41]

Slater-Hammel, A. T. (1955) Comparisons of reaction time measures to a visual stimulus and arm movement. *Res. Quart.*, 26, 470–479. [37]

Solley, W. H. (1951) Speed, accuracy or speed and accuracy as an initial directive in motor learning. *Motor skills research exchange*, 3, 47–51. [82]

Start, K. B. (1964) Kinaesthesia and mental practice. *Brit. J. Ed. Psych.*, 34, 85–90. [83]

Steel, W. I. (1952) The effect of mental practice on the acquisition of a motor skill. *J. Phys. Educ.*, 44, 101–108. [83]

Stout, G. F. (1899) *Manual of psychology*. London: Univ. Correspond. Coll. [76]

Stroud, J. M. (1955) The fine structure of psychological time. In H. Quastler (Ed.) *Information theory in psychology*. Illinois: Free Press. [30]

Sugerman, A. A. & Haronian, F. A. (1964) Body type and sophistication of body concept. *Journal of Personality*, 32, 3, 380–94. [98]

Swanton, E. W. *Obituary of G. F. Barnes*. London: *Daily Telegraph*, Dec. 27th 1967. [40]

Teichner, W. H. (1954) Recent studies of simple reaction time. *Psych. Bull.*, 51. [36]

Thorpe, W. H. (1956) *Learning and instinct in animals*. Cambridge: Harvard Univ. Press. [77]

Townsend, D. (1953) *The Oxford book of cricket coaching*. Oxford: Univ. Press. [13]

Twining, W. (1949) Mental practice and physical practice in learning a motor skill. *Res. Quart.*, 30, 432–435. [83]

Ulich, E. (1967) Some experiments in the function of mental training in the Acquisition of skills. *Ergonomics*, 10, 4, 411–419. [83]

Vandell, R. A., Davis, R. A., & Clugston, H. A. (1943) The function of mental practice in the acquisition of motor skills. *J. Gen. Psych.*, 29, 243–250. [82]

Vernon, M. D. (1965) *Psychology of perception*. London: Penguin Books. [16]

Vince, M. A. (1948a) Corrective movements in a pursuit task. *Q. J. Exp. Psych.*, 1, 85–103. [51]

Vince, M. A. (1948b) The intermittency of control movements and the psychological refractory period. *Brit. J. Psych.*, 38, 149–157. [10]

Warner, P. (1941) *The book of cricket*. London: Sporting Hand-books. [13]

Weaver, H. *A genius at 6' 5"*. London: *Observer* Oct. 24th, (1965) [70]

Welford, A. T. (1958) *Ageing and Human skill*. London: Oxford Univ. Press. [1]

Welford, A. T. (1960) The measurement of sensory-motor per-formance: survey and reappraisal of twelve years' progress. *Ergonomics*, 3, 189–230. [3]

Welford, A. T. (1967) Single channel operation in the brain. *Acta Psych.*, 27, 5–22. [52, 53]

Werner, A. C. (1958) Physical education and the development of leadership. College P. E. Assoc. Proceedings of 65th Annual Conf. New York. [90]

Weymouth, F. W. (1965) The eye as an optical instrument. In T. C. Ruch & H. D. Patton (Eds.) *Physiology and Biophysics*. London: Saunders. [64]

White, C. T. (1963) Temporal numerosity and the psychological unit of duration. *Psych. Mon.*, 77, 1–37. [30]

White, C. T. (1967) Eye, movements, evoked responses and visual perception: some speculations. *Acta Psych.*, 27, 337–340. [30]

Whiting, H. T. A. (1967) Visual motor coordination. Ph.D. Thesis, Dept. of Psych. Leeds Univ. [22, 81]

Whiting, H. T. A. (1968a) Training in a continuous ball-throwing, and catching task. *Ergonomics*, 11, 4, 375–382. [25, 84]

Whiting, H. T. A. (1969) An operational analysis of a continuous ball-throwing and catching task. *Ergonomics*, 12 (in press). [27]

Whiting, H. T. A. & Hendry, L. B. (1968b) A study of inter-national table-tennis players. Unpublished memorandum. [68, 95]

Wiener, N. (1948) *Cybernetics*. New York: Wiley. [6, 46]

Wilkinson, J. J. (1958) A study of reaction time measures to a kinaesthetic and a visual stimulus for a selected group of athletes and non-athletes. Doctor of P. E. thesis Indiana University. [37]

Winograd, S. (1942) The relationship of timing and vision to base-ball performance. *Res. Quart.*, 13, 481–493. [62]

Witkin, H., et al. (1954) *Personality through perception*. New York: Harper. [96, 97]

Witkin, H., et al. (1962) *Psychological differentiation*. New York: Wiley. [87, 96, 97]

Woodworth, R. S. (1958) *Dynamics of behaviour*. New York: Holt. [57]

Woodworth, R. S. & Schlosberg, H. (1963) *Experimental psych-ology*. London: Methuen. [36, 37, 44]

Zagora, E. (1959) Observations on the evolution and neuro-physiology of eye-limb coordination. *Opthalmol.*, 138, 241–254. [67]

Subject Index

Abilities, 99–101
Acceleration, 15, 17
Ambidextrality, 68–69
Anatomical unit, 52
Anticipation, 16, 18
Attention, 17
  selective, 4, 6, 76

Backswing, 49, 57
Badminton, 12, 56
Ball
  defined, 1
  trajectory, 24, 31, 34
  parabolic flight, 31
Ballistic
  movement, 10, 57, 58, 102
  strokes, 57
  actions, 58
Baseball, 13, 21–22, 42, 68, 81
Basketball, 13, 64, 70, 83
Batting skills, 9
Billiards, 56
Biophysical, 87
Biosocial, 86
Black-box model, 7
Body-type, 96, 98
Bowling, 39–40

Catching, 8, 22–34
Categories of ball skills, 8–9
Central nervous system, 60
Central vision, 70
Children, 17, 19, 44
Closure, 14, 22
Coaching, vii, 20
Compatability, 54, 57
Cricket, 13, 39–40, 43–44
Crossed lateral, 68

Cues, 19, 39
Cybernetics, 6

Deception, 8, 39
Decision
  making, 36–54, 61, 78
  mechanism, 52
  time, 38
Defensive game, 85
Demonstration, 75, 79
Depth perception, 65–67
Discrimination, 46, 57, 80
Display, 3, 4, 8, 29, 44, 47, 54
  compatible/incompatible, 47, 48
Dominance, 67–69
Downswing, 51
Dribbling, 70

Education, viii, 72
Effector mechanism, 3, 4, 55–56
Efferent information, 60–61
Exafference, 60
Experimental psychology, 14, 36
Extraversion, 87, 89, 97
Eye
  on the ball, 6, 12, 14, 22–35, 97
  angle subtended at, 16
  dominance, 67–71
  error sensing device, 15
  movements, 20–21, 34, 61
  muscles, 29

Feedback, 4, 5, 7, 16, 78, 80
  action, 6–8
  circuits, 15
  data, 4

Feedback—*cont.*
  information, 57
  internal and external, 7
  kinaesthetic, 79
  learning, 7
Field dependent/independent, 97–99
Figure-ground, 70, 98
Film loops, 75
Football, 9, 66, 69, 90
Forward swing, 49

Golf, 9, 90, 91
  swing, 12, 49, 50, 53
Good eye, 62
Grooving-in, 61
Group coaching, 85
Guidance, 80–81

Handedness, 67–69
Hereditary characteristics, 79, 104
Heterophoria, 64
Hinting, 80
Hockey, 81, 85

Imitation, 74–79
Inclusion principle, ix
Individual differences, 28, 84–101, 104
Input characteristics, 16–35, 55
  data, 2–3
  information, 57
Information, 3, 4, 7, 15, 57, 103
  chunks, 29
  computing, 11
  efferent, 60–61
  model, 57
  monitoring, 10, 20, 27
  outflow, 28
  positional, 16
  processing, 14–17
  proprioceptive, 3
  theory, 46
Inter-pupillary distance, 66–67

Kinaesthesia, 3, 14, 37, 56, 79, 100

Knowledge of results, 6–7
  augmented, 7

Lacrosse, 8
Lateral imbalance, 62
Limb dominance, 67–68

Maudsley Personality Inventory, 89
Mechanical principles, 19
Memory
  short-term, 75, 77
  permanent, 77
Mental image, 75
Mental practice, 82–83
Mesomorphy, 96
Models, 75, 80
  for skill, 2–5
Motor skill, 1
  units, 57
Movement time, 38, 41
Muscular system, 2

Nervous system, 58, 60, 79
Neuromuscular system, 49
Neuroticism, 87, 89

Oarsman, 58
Operational analysis, 40, 81
Orientation, 20
Orthophoria, 64
Outflow information, 60, 61
Output data, 2–3
  characteristics, 55–61

Perception, 4–6, 20, 62–67
  depth, 65–66
  and personality, 96–99
Perceptual
  motor skill, 1
  mechanisms, 3, 5
  moments, 30
  input, 60
  units, 30, 97
Peripheral vision, 69–71
Personality
  assessment, 85–89
  traits, 87, 99
  types, 87

Photography, 12, 20, 21
Plan, 58, 61, 76
Positional play, 54
Prediction, 22–28
Profiles, 88
Programmed, 51, 58
Progression-hypothesis, 17
 regression-hypothesis, 17
Proprioception, 3, 7, 51, 56, 57, 61
Psychophysical monism, 82

Reaction time, 36–48, 52, 54, 57, 70, 104
 simple, 36–41
 choice, 44–48
 transit, 41–42
 of children, 45
Reafference, 60
Reflex time, 38
Refractoriness, 48–54, 104
Replicability, 58–60
Rounders, 9
Rugby football, 93, 94

Selective
 attention, 4, 6, 76
 learning, 15
 perception, 6, 76
Sense organs, 5
Servomechanisms, 15–17
Setting-up, 48
Shaping, 78
Sight-screen, 16
Skill(s)
 batting, 9
 defined, 1
 open and closed, 9–10
 perceptual, 10, 21
 social, 1, 8
Skittles, 22
Snooker, 56
Social
 interaction, 85
 facilitation, 77
Soccer, 9, 66, 69, 90
Softball, 42
Sophistication of body-concept, 97

Spatial
 location, 60
 orientation, 61
Specificity, viii
Speed
 of ball, 42
 accuracy, 81–82
Squash, 13, 37, 48
Stereoscopic vision, 65
Strategy, 54, 79
Stress, 17
Systems,
 analysis defined, 2
 analysis in skill, 2–8

Table-tennis, 19, 48, 54, 68, 78, 85, 95
Target, 13, 55, 61
Tennis, 13, 14, 48, 64, 85, 89, 93, 98
 serve, 13, 56
 champions, 64
Throwing, 9, 70, 83
Timing, 11, 62
Tracking (ball), 21, 22
Training
 and education, viii, 72
 transfer of, viii–ix
 in ball skill, 19
Trajectory, 18, 24
Translatory mechanism, 3, 4, 5

Unorthodox players, 85

Velocity, 14–15, 28, 61
Vertical jump, 58
Vision, 55, 57, 62
 simultaneous, 62
Visual
 acuity, 62, 63, 64
 attention, 13, 22
 ability, 66
 apparatus, 34
 display, 39
 factors, 62–71
 information, 17
 pathway, 8
 system, 60
Volleyball, 64